WILLIAM S. SADLER:
CHAUTAUQUA'S MEDIC ORATOR

Dr. Vonne Meussling

With introductory material, index and illustrations by
John Bunker and Karen Pressler

WILLIAM S. SADLER: CHAUTAUQUA'S MEDIC ORATOR

Dr. Vonne Meussling

Republished in 2017 by B∪NKER PRESSLER BOOKS

Preliminary material, afterword, index ©2017
by John M. Bunker & Karen L. Pressler

Cover Art © John Bunker & Karen L. Pressler
Illustrations added for 2017 reproduction.

ISBN: 978-0-9885001-7-4
2017 Printing

B∪NKER PRESSLER BOOKS

"Two and a Guide"

Questions regarding this book can be addressed to:

B∪NKER PRESSLER BOOKS
8829 Heffelfinger Rd.
Churubusco, IN 46723

Email: bunker.pressler@gmail.com

Website: http://sites.google.com/site/edgarcayceandthehallofrecords/

TABLE OF CONTENTS

John's Introduction i
Karen's Introduction iii
THE THESIS v
   Abstract 3
   Acknowledgements 7
I. INTRODUCTION 9
   Statement of the Purpose 9
   Background Data 10
   Related Research 22
   Justification of the Study 23
   Design the Study 25
   Significant Sources 28
      Primary Sources. 28
      Summary 30
II. THE ORATOR 31
III. THE OCCASION 71
IV. THE AUDIENCE 101
V. THE SPEECH 134
      Dispositio 135
      Electio 140
      Inventio 147
      Ethos 148
      Pathos 155
      Logos 164
VI. SUMMATIONS AND CONCLUSIONS 176
   Summations 176
   Conclusions 182
   The orator. 183
   The occasion. 184
   The audience. 184
   The speech. 185
   Recommendations 186
BIBLIOGRAPHY 187

- A. PRIMARY SOURCES 187
  - 1. Papers and Letters 187
  - 2. Periodical Articles 188
  - 3. Books 193
- B. SECONDARY SOURCES 197
  - 1. Collected Documents 197
  - 2. Letters, Questionnaires, and Bulletins 197
  - 3. Unpublished Works 200
  - 4. Interviews 202
  - 5. Periodicals 202
  - 6. Books 213
  - 7. Newspapers 219
  - 8. Other Sources 220

VITA 221
About the Author 223
INDEX 227

John's Introduction

In the beginning of our search for information about the events leading up to the publication of the *Urantia Book*, which began in 1994, Karen and I traveled to Virginia Beach, Bowling Green University, Hopkinsville Kentucky, and Chicago, among other places. We were trying to piece together bits of information to develop an accurate account of past incidents linking Edgar Cayce with The *Urantia Book*. The trail was still fresh and some of the people connected with these events were still living, like Edgar Evans Cayce, Delbert D. Cayce III, Meredith and Irene Sprunger, and G. Vonne Meussling.

Dr. Meredith Sprunger, PhD, had talked to us much about Dr. William Sadler, MD, of Chicago, Illinois, who had been so involved with the development of the *Urantia Book*. We learned that Dr. Sadler had been the first doctor to speak publicly about health issues, during a time in history when such things were not permitted by the American Medical Association, before the days of radio and television. Most Americans learned about current events by reading newspapers. During this epoch in American history the word Chautauqua became a household word that was to change the country and then was to disappear as quickly as it came, about the time of the advent of automobiles and radio.

We discovered a doctoral thesis titled "William Sadler Chautauqua's Medic Orator," dated 1970, written by G. Vonne Meussling. We read her thesis and found it to be a gold mine of information. We thought that perhaps she might still have some records that she may have collected during the preparation of her thesis. We managed to contact her by telephone. To our disappointment, she told us that she had moved a couple of times since then and all of the records had been ruined by a flood in her basement. So that trail ended. By 1998, we published the first copy of *Edgar Cayce and the Urantia Book*.

John with Dr. Meussling

By the year 2016, we began to read the thesis again and decided that it would be good if it was available for people who were interested in the history of Dr. Sadler's life. We sought to contact Dr. Vonne Meussling again, who would now be 90 years old. Bowling Green State University was the first place we contacted. The alumni department was unable to help us. So we contacted other schools where she had been a teacher, but were unable to acquire her current whereabouts or even her photo. We were afraid that perhaps she was no longer living.

Then Karen managed to locate her son Mark and we contacted him. He told us she was alive and well and living in a nearby community! Mark helped us contact her and we set an appointment to meet with her. Dr. Meussling is a wonderful person, very kind and helpful to us in our effort to publish her thesis. We are happy to have the opportunity to introduce her to you!

John Bunker
Churubusco, IN 3/30/2017

Karen's Introduction

Our life has been such an adventure! It's been one of discovery, and learning, and meeting so many wonderful people. Thank goodness our interest was piqued at a time when so many resources were available to us, from living participants nearly a century old, to the electronic age of information sharing!

Most recently we met Dr. Vonne Meussling, a beautiful, vibrant woman, young at heart and optimistic about the future at 90! What a delight! John had spoken to her once on the phone two decades earlier regarding a book we were working on at the time, but we never stayed in touch.

Karen with Dr. Vonne Meussling

Her 1970 thesis, reprinted here, is a plethora of information about Dr. Sadler's early career as a medical orator. While portraying this lesser known facet of Dr. Sadler's professional life, Dr. Meussling has also presented a worthwhile history of the Chautauqua circuit in American history, along with insights into an overlooked period of advancement in the history of medical communication and understanding. She makes keen observations about life and morals in early twentieth century America. Dr. Sadler is rarely known for his substantial advances in public medical education and his enlightened recommendations of thought and attitude as significant paths to healing. He was eager to share his ideas with the public, but the rules established by the American Medical Association to prevent tricksters from taking advantage of them with questionable medical cures, were the same rules that prevented doctors from sharing important medical knowledge with the common man. This was a problem that Dr. Sadler was instrumental in reforming.

Our interest in Dr. Meussling's thesis was at its peak in the 1990's when we were trying to discover the "sleeping subject" involved with the inception of the *Urantia Book*. Any information about Dr. Sadler we could find at that time was valuable. As it turned out, Dr. Meussling's thesis was heavily used in our own work.

Now, years later, we realized that her unpublished work was nearing the end of its original copyright period, and could be a valuable resource if it was publicly available. Not knowing if Dr. Meussling was still living, we sought to locate her to obtain permission to republish it. After months of unsuccessful searching, we were ready to assume she was gone, but then we discovered that her son, Mark, worked in a local real estate office. He told us his mother was still alive and well, and gave us her contact information. She was happy to speak to us, and was enthusiastic about our republishing project. When we sat down to talk to her and showed her the first draft of our project, she laughingly said, *"This is amazing, this is absolutely amazing! That you have done this! Oh my. I can't believe it. So you know more about my thesis than I do!"*

Karen Pressler
Churubusco, IN 4/2/2017

THE THESIS

Dr. Meussling's thesis appears in its
entirety on the next pages.

Illustrations and an index were
added for this edition.

WILLIAM S. SADLER:
CHAUTAUQUA'S MEDIC ORATOR

(Original 1970 thesis with new illustrations)

Dr. Vonne Meussling

A Dissertation

**Submitted to the Graduate School of Bowling Green
State University in partial fulfillment of
the requirements for the degree of**

DOCTOR OF PHILOSOPHY

December 1970

Abstract

This study of William S. Sadler (1875-1969), physician, surgeon, psychiatrist, professor, and author of forty-two books, investigates that phase of his career devoted to oratory. It concentrates upon the period 1905 to 1926 when he was a popular lecturer on Chautauqua platforms. It traces the influences which molded his public speaking interest, from a high school commencement address delivered at the age of eight to the decision to become a public lecturer. This was unprecedented in an era when concepts of the American Medical Association did not permit doctors to advertise. He was a student of Sigmund Freud, an associate of Alfred Adler, Karl Jung and John Harvey Kellogg. These associations were evidenced as influential factors in his career.

The purpose of this study was to analyze rhetorically those elements of Sadler's speeches on preventive medicine, which governed his oral contributions. His message focused on the education of the masses so as to counteract public ignorance, medical quackery, and harmful patent remedies. The study revealed that audiences were eager for authentic health information.

Sadler had no published biography; however, the writer had access to his personal papers and books. Letters attesting to his popularity as a speaker were found in Special Collections at the University of Iowa. Early speeches were discovered at The John Crerar Library in Chicago.

Sadler would not be classified as a great orator; yet, he gained audience appeal through a unique style and implementation of histrionics and humor.

4

DEDICATION

A tribute to my mother

MARY IZETTA SITCLER

Whose example of perseverance and whose encouragement of excellence have always served as a source of inspiration for her daughter.

© G.Vonne Meussling 1970

All Rights Reserved

Acknowledgements

Special acknowledgement and appreciation is extended to my major professor, Dr. John T. Rickey, whose academic discipline has been a source of inspiration and guidance throughout my doctoral program.

A word of gratitude is also expressed to Professors Ray B. Browne, Raymond Yeager and Nelson R. Ober for their interest, advice, and assistance during this study.

Warm appreciation is conveyed to my husband, who has been too considerate to be acknowledged adequately, and to my children: Stephen, Mark, Vonne, and Todd, whose implicit confidence in their mother was a forceful impetus.

I. INTRODUCTION

For fifteen years William S. Sadler, a surgeon and psychiatrist, spoke to Chautauqua audiences across the country concerning "preventive medicine." It was his belief that the lay public had the inalienable right to be exposed to the latest medical knowledge in order to help themselves prevent illness and disease. He spoke in an era when established concepts of the American Medical Association did not permit doctors to advertise or to work for any organization that did. At the beginning of the twentieth century the public press was the primary media of information, but it did not carry columns on health. Sadler believed that oral discourse was an important tool in a democratic society; he used this tool to promote the popularization of physical hygiene and preventive medicine at the risk of being censured by the Medical Association for advertising. There are many facets to Sadler's career. He was an active surgeon, psychiatrist, professor, and author. Since this study will be confined to his speaking, it will refer to these other activities only insofar as they contribute to the understanding of him as a speaker.

Statement of the Purpose

The purpose of this study is to analyze rhetorically those elements of Sadler's speeches on preventive medicine, which governed his oral contributions to the American people between 1905 and 1926. In this critical process the methodology employed will be based upon the traditional components of analysis: the orator, the occasion, the audience, and the speech.

Background Data

It should be possible to assess Sadler's audiences by reviewing the literature. The insights into the customs, attitudes, beliefs, and needs of the people in his audiences will provide criteria for the measurement of Sadler's relevance and adaptiveness, and will offer a primary basis for the justification of the study.

By today's standards, few citizens in the first quarter of the twentieth century had the advantages of higher education. In fact," ... it was not until 1918 that all forty - eight states adopted compulsory education; even at that time most states began by requiring only two or three years' attendance at a grammar school."[1] Before the beginning of the radio in 1920,[2] Americans derived most of their knowledge of national and world affairs from the newspapers. "Each city of any size relied primarily for its news on papers which were published locally and gave considerable attention to local events."[3] The tremendous appeal of the traveling Chautauquas resulted from a combination of the American's thirst for sophisticated information, for entertainment, and the absence of other means by which such information might be acquired. Thus, the Chautauquas served primarily to make a social, cultural, and educational contribution to the people of rural America. Sadler saw the need and decided to use this opportunity to teach health education.

---

[1] Henry Bamford Parkes and Vincent P. Carosso Crescent, *America: A History, Book One: 1900 - 1933* (New York, 1963), p. 91.

[2] Ward L. Quaal and Leo A. Martin, *Broadcast Management* (New York, 1969), p. 41.

[3] Ibid, p. 95.

A brief review of health statistics between 1900 and today indicates the situational factors of this era. Life tables for the United States covering the years 1900 - 1902 indicate a life expectancy for white males of 48.2, for white females of 51.1; nonwhites had life expectancy predictions of approximately twelve years 1ess.[5] Cleanliness had become one of the primary postulates in the nineteenth and twentieth centuries. Early superstitions in the belief that the frequent use of soap was harmful to the skin and the religious dogma that related the custom of undressing for bathing to the original sin, had overdeveloped modesty.[6] Thomlinson reported that medical science made great advances against the ravages of disease in the last fifty to one

---

[4] Redpath tent - Redpath Chautauqua Bureau Records, Special Collections Department, University of Iowa Libraries (Iowa City).

[5] Ralph Thomlinson, *Population Dynamics: Causes and Consequences of World Demographic Change* (New York, 1965), p. 117. Hereafter cited as Thomlinson, *Population*.

[6] Henry Sigerist, M.D., *Civilization and Disease* (Ithaca, New York, 1944), p. 27.

hundred years but was only a rudimentary art prior to that time.[7] James B. Conant, in 1952, wrote: "It is probable that only within this century have medical men and surgeons helped more people than they have injured -- one might almost say, cured more persons than they have killed."[8]

As late as 1883, the Secretary of the Wisconsin State Board of Health wrote: "I do not know how the impression has gone abroad, as it has, that we have a law regulating the practice of medicine, for we have none."[9] It was said in regard to the status of medicine in the United States in the nineteenth century that for all practical purposes "anybody was a 'doctor' who called himself a doctor."[10] "Thus, the ill person left uncured by home remedies and local 'Hippos,' often placed his trust in the promises of elixirs, extracts, balms, and pills."[11] A feeling of ambivalence toward the medical profession was prevalent in the United States. "Doctors can receive worshipful respect and round denunciation in almost the same breath."[12] Medical research was far more advanced than medical training. It was not until the 1910's and 1920's when Abraham Flexner exposed the primitive and scandalous quackery prevalent in medical education in the publication of a report to the Carnegie

---

[7] Thomlinson, *Population*, p. 95.
[8] James B. Conant, *Modern Science and Modern Man* (Garden City, 1952), p. 129.
[9] Madge E. Pickard and Carlyle Buley, *The Midwest Pioneers: His Ills, Cures, and Doctors* (New York, 1946), p. 262. Hereafter cited as Pickard and Buley, *Midwest Pioneers*.
[10] Ibid.
[11] Ibid, p. 268.
[12] Oliver Garceau, "Morals of Medicine," *The Annals of the American Academy of Political and Social Science*, CCCLXIII (January, 1966), 61. Hereafter cited as Garceau, "Morals of Medicine."

Foundation, that sweeping reforms closed nearly one hundred inadequate medical schools.[13]

There was great progress in medical science in the second half of the nineteenth and in the beginning of the twentieth centuries for the control of communicable diseases.[14] But knowledge alone was not enough; in order to utilize this knowledge, the people needed, to be educated. The need for health education and for capable teachers was considerable:

> *Medicine already is sufficiently advanced to give the physician the means necessary for the practice of preventive medicine on a large scale. Prevention of disease must become the goal of every physician whatever his status may be. The barriers between preventive and curative medicine must be broken down.*[15]

Since medicine was sufficiently advanced, it appears that the above problem could easily be corrected if medical doctors were willing to communicate to the lay public concerning preventive medicine.

In the consideration of communication through the media of public speaking, Thonssen and Baird have suggested that we review the sociological and psychological setting of the times:

---

[13] Thomlinson, *Population*, p. 96.
[14] Henry E. Sigerist, *Medicine and Human Welfare* (New Haven, Connecticut, 1941), p. vii. This is from the Terry Lectures at Yale University, 1940. Hereafter cited as Sigerist, *Medicine*.
[15] Ibid. p. 143.

> *Since every judgment of a public speech contains a historical constituent, the critic is peculiarly concerned with determining the nature of the setting in which the speaker operated.... It cannot be overemphasized that speeches are events occurring in highly complex situations;* ...[16]

In 1905 the situation was complex for a medical doctor who wanted to speak to the lay public concerning health matters because the American Medical Association believed that it was a "debatable enterprise of physicians engaging in public-health educational efforts."[17] The association recognized the value and the need of educating the public but they wanted a reputable profession and "some features of codes of professional ethics are common to all professions. A universal rule is that against advertising."[18] The fact is that the American Medical Association did not permit doctors to speak to lay audiences on medical topics because they equated speaking with advertising.

---

[16] Lester Thonssen and A. Craig Baird, *Speech Criticism* (New York, 1948), p. 312. Hereafter cited as Thonssen and Baird, *Speech Criticism*.

[17] Willim S. Sadler, "Psychiatric Educational Work" (paper read at the Ninety - second Annual Meeting of the American Psychiatric Association, May 4-8, 1936, St. Louis, Missouri). Hereafter cited as Sadler, "Psychiatric Educational Work."

[18] A. N. Carr Saunders, *Professions: Their Organization and Place in Society* (Oxford, 1928), pp. 3 - 31, in Howard M. Vollmer and Donald L. Mills (eds.), *Professionalization* (New Jersey: Prentice-Hall, 1966), p. 6.

AMA Headquarters, Chicago, 1902

The rule which forbade doctors to be connected with any business that advertised was a very stringent one. The code of ethics of the Chicago Medical Society will be reviewed for the specific reason that the speaker of this study was a member of this society and Chicago was the area in which he operated. In effect the code was:

> *Identical with the code of the national association, it has as its objectives the upholding of the dignity of the profession, the protection of physicians and public against unscientific doctrines and ideas, and the prevention of a commercial-type competition among doctors. The weapons which the Chicago Medical Society might use to enforce standards of professional behavior were those of similar groups everywhere; social pressure and the power of expulsion from organized medicine. The hostility of the local profession was a hazard to professional reputation and success which few physicians would dare*

> to risk ... *Occasionally a member was dropped for advertising.*[19]

Even though a Speaker's Bureau of the American Medical Association was established in January, 1911,[20] a doctor still was not allowed to be associated with any other organization that advertised if it were not connected with the General Medical Society. In a paper delivered to the American Psychiatric Association in 1936, Sadler recalled the one time reluctance of physicians to speak to lay audiences:

> *This reluctance was only overcome by the request of the President of Chicago Medical Society that we give some talks under the auspices of the Society on Saturday evenings to lay audiences in one of the assembly rooms of the Public Library. This was the first official attempt [1911] of the Society to participate in the then debatable enterprise of physicians' engaging in public - health educational efforts.*[21]

---

[19] Thomas Neville Bonner, *Medicine in Chicago 1850-1950* (Madison: The American Historical Research Center, Inc., 1957), p. 210.

[20] James B. Burrow, *AMA: Voice of American Medicine* (Baltimore: John Hopkins Press, 1963), pp. 45 - 46. "After the Los Angeles session of 1911, the Council of Health and Public Instruction inaugurated a wider program of work. Stating as its principal mission, 'the development of public confidence in the purposes and work of the American Medical Association and of the profession,' it planned ... the organization of a speaker's bureau...."
"The Speaker's Bureau, established January 1, 1911, to provide a list of physicians throughout the nation capable of speaking at public meetings that the profession sponsored, proved usually successful... Seventeen months after the establishment of the bureau, 64 speakers had accepted appointment to the panel.... The list of speakers registered with the bureau had increased to 255 by June, 1917, but the expense fund provided by the Association had been discontinued the preceding year, and each society requesting a speaker then assumed responsibility for paying traveling expense."

[21] Sadler, "Psychiatric Educational Work," p. 1.

In 1905, a young medical student, William S. Sadler, gave a speech entitled "Americanitis, or the High Pressure Life." His theme was, "You must learn the art of living with yourself as you are and the world as it is."[22] Sadler believed in talking to people to help cure their ills; he not only believed in face - to - face communication, but also in public communication.

After graduation from Cooper Medical College in San Francisco, Medical Department of Leland Stanford University, Sadler became more and more concerned that too many pills were being given *after* people became ill and too little was being done to prevent illnesses from occurring. Hesitant at first, the young physician eventually concluded that this was an issue for which his temperament and talent motivated him.[23]

In 1906, Dr. William Lowe Bryan, President of Indiana University at Bloomington, offered Sadler a position as head of the medical department at the University. Although he had signed the contract and had leased a house, the night before he was to move to the University, he decided that he could do more for humanity if he were free to give lectures and to write books on the adaptation to life and the maintenance of mental and physical health.[24]

However, much more than the decision to make public speaking a part of his career was involved. Even though he, as a medical man, deemed it his duty to promote the popularization of preventive medicine, there existed two apparent factors: a considerable prejudice against health

---

[22] This theme is expressed repetitively in Sadler's speeches and books.
[23] Sadler's Personal Papers. (MSS in office and home, 533 Diversey Parkway, Chicago.). Hereafter cited as Sadler's Papers.
[24] Sadler's Papers.

propaganda and a risk to his professional reputation.

Sadler was taking a calculated risk when he tried to attain a spot on the Chautauqua lecture platform in 1907; not only might he be censured by having his name removed from the professional register which would limit his practice, but censuring might prevent his association with other colleagues. His need to speak to the lay public had to be balanced with his need to preserve his professional reputation.

It was not easy for Sadler to get a place on the program of the Chautauqua circuit because there was no precedent for the medical lectures that he proposed. When he first talked to the manager of the Redpath Chicago circuit to tell him about the health lectures that he would like to present, "the manager looked at me and said he couldn't think of anything nearer zero for a Chautauqua audience than health lectures, and if he ever planned to consider such a move he certainly wouldn't pick me to do it."[25] Sadler was refused a contract; however he had determination. He believed in "giving precedence to essentials, "and to him the theme of mental and physical health was essential. During the following year, he gave some health lectures in small towns a safe distance from Chicago. The manager of the Redpath Chautauqua circuit, always looking for new talent, heard him and in the following year he sought Sadler to sign a contract.[26]

> But we [wife and registered nurse] finally made the grade and gave our sample performance in 1907 in Appleton, Wisconsin. There was no first aid in those

---

[25] Ibid.
[26] William S. Sadler, *Americanitis - Blood Pressure and Nerves* (New York, 1925), p. 75. Hereafter cited as Sadler, *Americanitis*.

> days such as now taught by the Red Cross. The Lyceum [Chautauqua] sent scouts to hear and see the various lectures and performances, and the Sadlers' performance at Appleton was picked for the ensuing season. Three years later I sat in the same manager's office and signed a contract for the biggest money that had ever been paid for Chautauqua performers with the exception of William Jennings Bryan.[27]

When Sadler addressed the Ninety - second Annual Meeting of the American Psychiatric Association in 1936, he reminisced:

> I recall with what trepidation some of us, thirty years ago, first presumed to address lay audiences on health subjects. At that time the public press did not carry health columns with questions and answers, and physicians were not in the habit of addressing lay audiences on health subjects. My wife and professional co - laborer, Dr. Lena K. Sadler, shared with me this urge to educate the layman in health matters, and soon after graduating in medicine we began to give lectures in cities somewhat removed from Chicago; but the fear of being suspected of doing something unethical or possibly of being accused of advertising was sufficient to keep us from lecturing in Chicago for five or six years.[28]

In 1911 Sadler left his lecturing to study in Europe under Sir Berkley Moynahan in Leeds, and under Sigmund Freud at Vienna. Sadler had always been interested in psychiatry because he hypothesized that the inability to adapt to life situations actually caused "mental mischief" which eventually led to physical illness. During his year in Vienna, many Friday evenings were spent in Freud's apartment where he

---

[27] Sadler's Papers.
[28] Sadler, "Psychiatric Educational Work," p. 1.

engaged in informal discussions with Freud, Adler, and Jung concerning psychiatry and psychological theories.[29] Sadler supported more and more the theory of mind cure; he believed in talking to people and giving them verbal confidence. He was certain that the therapy of words could instill confidence in patients' recuperative abilities. He stated in a book first published in 1912:

> And so patent medicines, placebos, and quack doctors have largely cured their patients because of the confidence they inspired, the faith they generated, the assurance they gave, their glowing promises, and their unqualified guarantee to cure.[30]

Sadler staunchly felt that the *modus operandi* of the mind could be a factor in preventive medicine. Noting that professional practitioners often effected remarkable cures, Sadler advocated greater involvement of the medical profession in the psychological factors surrounding functional illnesses. Mind cure was a prevailing theme in most of Sadler's speaking and writing. He believed that:

> Human health and happiness cannot be greatly promoted if the civilized races do not bear in mind two great truths: first, the influence of the mind the prevention of disease; second, the marvelous power of nature to heal.[31]

From the above, it may be surmised that a problem existed

---

[29] Sadler's Papers.
[30] William S. Sadler, *The Psychology of Faith and Fear* (Chicago, 1912), p. 103. Hereafter cited as Sadler, *The Psychology of Faith and Fear*.
[31] William Sadler and Lena K. Sadler, *The Truth About Mental Healing* (Chicago, 1938), p. 154. Hereafter cited as Sadler, *The Truth About Mental Healing*.

in the early part of the twentieth century for a medical doctor who held a strong commitment toward public health education. Even though Sadler felt the urgency to attempt to change or modify prevalent attitudes, biases, and behavior patterns which restricted the health and the longevity of a considerable segment of the American people, the restrictions of the professional medical codes produced a calculated risk for him. However, he decided to give public health speeches since "he had to live with himself as he was and the world as it was."[32] Thus, his courage and his deep convictions motivated him to speak "... in common words the needs and hopes of common people." [33]

---

[32] Theme repeated in Sadler's books and speeches.
[33] William Norwood Brigance, "Effectiveness of the Public Platform," *Annals of American Academy of Political and Social Science* (March, 1947), p. 72.

Related Research

In reviewing indices in the *Quarterly Journal of Speech* and *Speech Monographs,* the *Dissertation Abstracts* and *American Doctoral Dissertations,* no specific research has been discovered concerning the oratory of a physician - psychiatrist in the field of speech. Two related dissertations have been done concerning the health reform movement: William B. Walker wrote a doctoral dissertation in 1955 at Johns Hopkins University on "The Health Reform Movement in the United States -- 1830 - 1870," and in 1962 Jonathan Gunther Penner wrote a dissertation concerning the "Public Speaking in the Health Reform Movement in the United States ---1863 - 1943." This latter dissertation did not appear to be an exhaustive study; for example, Dr. Woods Hutchinson, one of the first professional doctors who lectured on health improvement through nutrition, was not mentioned. Dr. Sadler's name was not mentioned even though evidence of his early speaking is documented in the Chautauqua history books. The only professional doctor named was Dr. John Harvey Kellogg, health lecturer on dietary and hygienic habits. Richard W. Schwarz wrote a dissertation at the University of Michigan in 1964 on the "Life of John Harvey Kellogg"; this study was a biography in the field of history.

The above data indicates a need for a study such as undertaken here. Walker's dissertation documented the continuing need for health reform and health education. Penner analyzed rhetorically the speaking of one doctor who lectured on preventive medicine through proper dietary habits. Schwarz's biographical study is closely related as Sadler started work at the age of fourteen as a bell boy in the Battle Creek Sanitarium under the direction of Kellogg In 1895, Sadler was sent to Chicago and was appointed an administrator of one of Dr. Kellogg's most ambitious social service projects, the Chicago Medical Mission.[34] Sadler was an important figure in this movement and was one of the primary sources of information for Schwarz's study.

Justification of the Study

Since there is not a single inclusion of doctors in the three - volume *A History and Criticism of American Public Address*, sponsored by the Speech Association of America, one might infer that the doctor has had little significance in our society in the field of oratory. It appears that the students of public address have neglected the area of the medical profession.

This study is not intended as an attempt to expand the theory of speech, but as a study of the adaptation of present theory to the spreading of medical knowledge.

The following considerations are the rationale for studying Sadler's speaking in the field of Public Address:

1. Sadler was a pioneer of his day. His deliberate efforts to reach large audiences to bring the message of health was unprecedented for a man of the medical profession. Through his public speaking he helped to focus attention on some of the vital health issues of the day.[35]

---

[34] Caroline Louise Clough, *His Name Was David* (Washington, D.C., 1955), p. 65. Hereafter cited as dough, *His Name Was David*.
[35] Harry P. Harrison and Karl Detzer, *Culture Under Canvas: The Story of Tent Chautauqua* (New York, 1958), p. 47. Writers of Chautauqua history indicate that Sadler had a widespread impact on Chautauqua audiences. Chautauqua audiences, had developed the practice of showing audience appreciation on Sundays (when they did not think

2. The importance of public oratory in a democratic society and its particular force in the history of medicine may be reflected in the career of William S. Sadler.

While it is not always possible to measure an orator's influence, some indication of Sadler's effectiveness has been reported in Chautauqua histories:

Sadler Day was an important occasion on any Chautauqua. Dr. William and Dr. Lena with the aid of a nurse gave helpful first - aid demonstrations, the nurse playing the part of the patient.... The Chautauqua talent usually "doubled in brass," as the old circus saying puts it.[36]

In speaking to audiences concerning the immediate needs of their day, he had an influence in improving the quality of the life of man and of society. We cannot assess him by his fame because he did not have fame but "Fame, in and of itself, is not proof of influence ... Perhaps the frequently mentioned speech or person was less influential than a seldom mentioned speech or person."[37]

---

it appropriate to applaud) by a gesture which became known as the Chautauqua Salute -- a waving of handkerchiefs. One historian writes: "For decades the practice of waving handkerchiefs persisted. Not until just before the First World War did a Chicago doctor, lecturing on a Chautauqua circuit on causes of the common cold, finally succeed in putting a stop to the practice." "Dr. William Sadler was a psychiatrist. Fortunately for chautauqua, he respected the germ theory as much as he did Freud; it was he who, after one startling experience with the 'Chautauqua salute,' drove it out of business."

[36] Gay MacLaren, *Morally We Roll Along* (Boston, 1938), p. 147. Hereafter cited as NacLaren, *Morally We Roll Along*.

[37] Ernest C. Bormann, *Theory and Research in the Communicative Arts* (New York, 1966), p. 238. Hereafter cited as Bormann, *Research*.

Since his impact upon the forces around him came significantly through his oratory, Sadler deserves a place in the tradition of "a good man speaking well."

Design the Study

In order to view the social context and the relationship of Sadler's speeches to the world in which he lived, this study will use the historical - critical method of research. The historical - critical approach is commonly defined as: "The study of a period, person, or phenomenon in human development in order to record discovered facts in an accurate, coherent, and critical narrative that posits causations and probabilities."[38] The historical - critical design will synthesize the following elements: (1) facets of the speaker's biography that are relevant to his career as a speaker -- associations and causal relationships that contributed to his training as a speaker; (2) the extrinsic factors -- those elements exterior to the speech -- such as the times, the setting, the audience, and the occasion; (3) the issues which were the principal concern of the, message; (4) the intrinsic factors -- the internal components of the message communicated. These factors include the arrangement, the style, and the invention; and (5) the assessment of the speaker. Bormann suggested the rationale for including these elements.

The critic needs to study the speaker, particularly his speech training and intellectual development; the critic needs to study the audience, and he needs to study the occasion. The critic needs to understand these elements

---

[38] J. Jeffrey Auer, *An Introduction to Research in Speech* (New York, 1959), p. 28.

before he examines the speech and tries to explain its nature.[39]

If, as Cicero and later classical rhetoricians proposed, "the style is the man," and if the effectiveness of a speaker can be measured and assessed by his total personality, then biographical considerations, if chosen for their rhetorical significance, can acquaint the reader with the man as a speaker. Hillbruner said, "... the words themselves, as they come to the audience ... are inherently part of him; they come from his life."[40]

Chapter I, *Introduction,* presents the purpose and overview of the study. Chapter II, *The Orator,* introduces the subject of the research. This chapter presents a biographical picture of Sadler set in the matrix of his early life environment. It reviews those events which may have influenced his career, especially his decision to become a public lecturer. Influences of family, environment, education, and significant others are evaluated; personal, professional, and rhetorical influences which contributed to his emergence as a speaker are examined. This chapter finds a correlation between his message and his background in the choice of content as well as in the manner of delivery. The history of Sadler's public service career plus other relevant biographical data is sketched in the effort to qualify the orator as a man of sincerity and good will.

Chapter III, *The Occasion,* provides an in - depth representation of the character and quality of the Chautauqua platforms. Because the Chautauqua appeal was based upon

---

[39] Bormann, *Research,* p. 233.
[40] Anthony Hillbruner, *Critical Dimensions: The Art of Public Address* (New York, 1966), p. 44. Hereafter cited as Hillbruner, *Dimensions.*

a very distinctive type of program, its talent can be considered only by that distinctiveness. Supporting the conservative norms of rural and small - town America, Chautauqua managers took more than an incidental interest in the personal beliefs and opinions of their lecturers. Sadler's success on the Chautauqua circuits can only be appreciated when the peculiar requirements of that platform are known.

Chapter IV, *The Audience,* surveys the demographic, sociological, and psychological characteristics of the typical Chautauqua audience; it also reviews the historical events responsible for major social change in this period. This chapter shows that the times, the audiences, and the occasions do mold the speaker's Ideas and style. The public address critic is obligated to evaluate the nature of a specific audience at a critical juncture in history.[41]

It is maintained that the nature of Sadler's message involved him with more personal habits and opinions than would be the case with political orators and others. To be effective at that level of communication, Sadler had to develop confidence and trust in his audience; this could only be done by adaptation to the needs of the audience. His *ethos* became crucial to his success. Acknowledging the norms of Chautauqua ideals and traditions, Sadler gained the respect of his auditors; by adapting his style to their expectations he held their attention; by avoiding the use of medical jargon while employing simple terms and ordinary illustrations he made effective communication.

This chapter demonstrates Sadler's versatility as an orator. It suggests that his primary message remained the same but

---

[41] Hillbruner, *Dimensions*, p. 29.

that the changing social, economic, and political conditions of the American people demanded creative adaptation to keep the message viable. It concludes that the timeliness of Sadler's speeches may be the reason that they cannot be considered timeless.

Chapter V, *The Speech*, offers a rhetorical analysis of a typical speech. The speech, "What Every Salesman Should Know About His Health," is from a stenographically recorded lecture session. Because a critic "must be concerned with determining the nature of the setting in which the speaker operated"[42] and because "oratory functions within the framework of public affairs,"[43] this chapter serves to integrate the various components of the speaking situation; it is concerned with the occasion, the audience, the message, and the response. The canons of classical rhetoric are used to divide the analysis into *dispositio, inventio, electio, memoria,* and *pronunciatio*.

Chapter VI, *Summations and Conclusions*, summarizes the findings of the previous chapters, reviewing the overall significance of Sadler's public speaking career. The conclusions outline the merits of this particular study and suggest additional areas for related research.

Significant Sources

<u>Primary Sources.</u> The pursuit of this study was made possible through the cooperation of Dr. Sadler's daughter, Christy Sadler, who graciously shared her father's private papers and books with the writer. To date, there is no published

---

[42] Thonssen and Baird, Speech Criticism, p. 312.
[43] Ibid, p. 315.

biography of his life except for brief synopses in *Who's Who* and *Who's Who in The Midwest*. The primary sources of information include the following:

1. Dr. Sadler's personal unpublished papers.

2. Dr. Sadler's forty - two published works.

3. Dr. Sadler's unpublished class lectures.

4. Dr. Sadler's numerous publications of periodical articles.

5. Dr. Sadler's manuscripts of speeches.

6. Interviews with Christy Sadler, his daughter, other members of his family, his personal secretary of seventeen years, and his friends.

7. Interviews with individuals who sat in Sadler's audiences.

8. Newspaper accounts of his speeches from various states.

9. Mail responses of former students solicited by the writer; one hundred forty - six letters were sent.

10. Authentic programs and brochures of Chautauqua publicity.

11. The author's personal observation of Sadler in a speaking situation.

Summary

At the beginning of the twentieth century the lay public did not have the advantages of the mass media that we have today; most of the national and world affairs information was obtained from local newspapers. Even though medical science was making great advances against common illnesses and communicable disease, the lay public often remained uninformed. The need for health education, the need for capable teachers to teach the people about preventive medicine was imperative.

The American Medical Association, attempting as it was in the early 1900's to strengthen the standards and ethics of the profession, had raised strong opposition to any method of public information which suggested advertising. One might conclude that, in its efforts to legitimize the medical profession, the association overreacted.

The purpose of this study is to analyze rhetorically those elements of Sadler's speeches on preventive medicine which governed his oral contributions to the American people between 1905 and 1926. In this critical process the methodology employed will be based upon the traditional rhetorical components of the orator, the occasion, the audience, and the speech.

II. THE ORATOR

William Samuel Sadler was born in Spencer, Indiana, to Samuel Cavins Sadler and Sarah Isabelle (Wilson) Sadler on June 24, 1875. His father was a graduate of the Chicago Conservatory of Music; he was a teacher and a performer.

Preparation for becoming an orator began early in young Sadler's life. While living in Wabash, Indiana, he spent much time listening to a relative, General McNaught, one-time Chief of scouts to General U. S. Grant, tell stories about the Civil War. Further exposure to history came from General Lew Wallace, a close neighbor, who was at the time writing *Ben Hur*. Sadler was fortunate to have Wallace's history books in which to look at pictures of battles and to read as much as a boy of eight could comprehend. He possibly was preparing his first speech as he thought about history and entertained himself by laying out battle plans in his back yard.[44]

His first informal speaking opportunity came while at a family reunion. For entertainment, General McNaught asked him if he would like to give a speech on the battles of history. A rain barrel was the platform for his first discourse. NcNaught was amazed at his tremendous apperception.[45] Through associates of General McNaught, Sadler received the opportunity to deliver his first formal speech at the age of eight. Addressing a high school commencement in Indianapolis, Indiana, on "The Crucial Battles of History," his public speaking career was launched.[46]

---

[44] Sadler's Papers.
[45] Statement by Christy Sadler, personal interview, December 29, 1969. Hereafter cited as Christy Interview.
[46] Sadler's Papers.

A few years later, while searching through the attic when he was twelve, he found an old Bible. Thinking about the old deserted church across the tracks from his house, he called his baseball buddies together and for several afternoons they "played church," i.e., his gang was the audience and he was the speaker. This small beginning of preaching in a vacated pulpit had its reverberations as he continued to prepare himself for a career of public speaking.[47]

Sadler's mother would not allow him to attend the public schools following the death of his sister because she was afraid that he might contract a communicable disease; thus, he received most of his formal education from his parents, tutors, and through his own initiative.[48]

At the age of fourteen, Sadler left his home in Wabash, Indiana, and moved to Battle Creek, Michigan. He worked as a bell boy in the world renowned Battle Creek Sanitarium headed by Dr. John Harvey Kellogg and attended Battle Creek College. Dr. John Harvey Kellogg was influential in molding the lives of many young people. "In those days he did much toward giving needed counsel, direction, and even financial assistance to ... young men who were struggling to get ahead."[49] Kellogg was to have more than a passing influence on the life of Sadler.

At the college Sadler 'organized a group of boys to study rhetoric under a Professor Bell. In order to study Latin, he organized another class under the direction of Professor Percy McGann; this class met at 5:00 am, before work

---

[47] Ibid.
[48] Statement by Dr. Meredith Sprunger, personal interview, April 24, 1970. Hereafter cited as Sprunger Interview.
[49] Clough, p. 49.

started at the sanitarium. Sadler had a propensity for organizational techniques which can be observed throughout his career.

During this time when he was sixteen and was visiting a church in Fort Wayne, Indiana, the minister extended an open invitation to the laity to speak; Sadler impulsively accepted the opportunity. After church the minister called him into his study and inquired concerning his knowledge of the Bible. The minister was planning a two - week vacation; he asked Sadler to preach for him during his absence. Sadler was eager to speak and for two weeks he preached both morning and evening sermons. He received letters of commendation concerning these efforts; a local newspaper called him "the boy preacher."[50] His preaching as a boy possibly led to his later decision to enter the ministry.

On March 7, 1899, he became a licensed minister of the Seventh Day Adventist Church, and in 1901 he became an ordained minister.[51] However, he rarely revealed this facet of his career to his closest associates. In his youth, Sadler did not remain with one career for long; he adapted to new situations easily and was willing to apply his energies to new tasks.

When William K. Kellogg, Harvey's brother, began the manufacture of health foods in 1893, Sadler was asked to be salesman and to present these foods to the grocery trade. In 1894, at the age of nineteen, Sadler began to demonstrate the use of health food. He became successful and did so well at the selling profession that the factory had difficulty filling his orders.[52] Undoubtedly Sadler drew

---

[50] Sadler's Papers.
[51] Ministerial License, Certificate of Ordination in Sadler's papers.
[52] Sadler's Papers.

upon this phase of his career for techniques in dealing with competitors, and it provided personal illustrations of how to attain sales from clientele. He was later to recall this authoritative information in his speech, 'What Every Salesman Should Know About His Health."

While at Battle Creek, Sadler combined his organizational abilities and a penchant for detective work by forming the Young Men's Intelligence Society. This was to lead to an interesting addition to the broadening experiences of his early career. Working in association with the Comstock Society for the Suppression of Vice and with United States Post Office Inspectors, Sadler figured predominantly in a number of successful exposures of illicit printers and purveyors of porno-graphic literature in the city of Chicago.[53]

In 1895, Dr. John Harvey Kellogg, founder of the Chicago Medical Mission, sent Sadler to Chicago to be secretary of the medical mission. This mission was operated by the International Medical Missionary and Benevolent Society. There were approximately a dozen centers of activity in the city that were under the direction of the mission. Some of these were the Mission Training School, Life Boat Mission, Free Dispensary affiliated with Pacific Garden Mission, Working Men's Home, Day Nurseries, Chicago's first free baths, and the News Boys' Club.[54] In addition to his executive responsibilities, Sadler was the initiator of a magazine called *The Life Boat*. For six years he edited this magazine that reported the accounts of the Mission; the circulation reached 150,000.[55]

---

[53] Ibid.
[54] Clough, p. 65.
[55] Ibid, p. 100.

During the years that he worked with the "skid row," Sadler developed insights concerning human behavior. When he periodically returned to Battle Creek, the gymnasium would be filled with nurses and workers of the sanitarium in order to hear his inspiring accounts of the work with the outcasts of Chicago. His personal papers mentioned that "everyone who heard him was inspired with the spirit of 'onward,' and of 'making that which is, what it ought to be.'"[56] Many years later he gave lectures on the Chautauqua circuit concerning the life of those unfortunates who lived in the city slums.

While Sadler was working with the Chicago Medical Mission, Dr. Kellogg felt it necessary that he receive more evangelistic instruction. He therefore enrolled as a special student at Moody Bible Institute.

In 1897, Sadler married Lena Kellogg, the niece of Dr. John Harvey Kellogg. In 1899 their first son was born, but lived only nine months. While comforting his wife, Sadler said, "You can have another baby, and perhaps in the meantime since you have always wanted to do it, we can study medicine."[57]

They entered Cooper Medical College in San Francisco in 1901. While at Cooper they earned their room and board by operating a home for Christian medical students; they also tutored students in chemistry. Kellogg urged them to return to Chicago to finish their studies. Thus, Sadler and his wife returned to Chicago and matriculated in the University of Chicago (Rush Medical College) to finish their medical training. While finishing his medical work, Sadler

---

[56] Sadler's Papers.
[57] Sadler's Papers.

paid his expenses by lecturing and by special detective work.[58]

Again, he demonstrated a talent for this type of activity. Largely through his services, a wide - scale situation of graft in Chicago politics was exposed.[59] Many years later, he reflected how this work had almost led him into an entirely different career than the one he followed. He had been offered an executive position in the governmental intelligence organization which eventually was to become the Federal Bureau of Investigation.[60]

In 1925 he inscribed his book, *Americanitis,* to his wife, "to my dear wife and co - laborer -- who first listened to this lecture 20 years ago -- with love and best wishes -- W.S.S."[61] In 1906, they both graduated from medical school and began their medical practice together. The Sadlers' were not only husband and wife, but also were business associates. They had adjoining offices. They performed operations together and worked as a team.[62]

In December 1907, their second son, William Samuel, Jr., was born. As will be shown later, Sadler's family participated in many of his activities; however, it was his leadership and organizational ability which established the character of his multi - faceted career. Yet, Sadler did not care for the limitations of institutional management.

---

[58] Ibid.
[59] Ibid.
[60] Sprunger Interview.
[61] Sadler, *Americanitis,* inscription inside front cover.
[62] Statement by Anna Rawson personal secretary of Dr. Sadler for seventeen years, personal interview, December 30, 1969. Hereafter cited as Rawson Interview.

Several individuals sought Sadler's organizational ability; Dr. David Paulson requested his help in the organization of the Hinsdale Sanitarium. A Guggenheim family was interested in establishing a combination sanitarium and hotel in a northern Chicago suburb. They offered to spend six million dollars for the institution and would have given the Sadlers fifty - one per cent of the stock, had they administered the operation. However, the contract stated that full - time work must be given to the institution. Sadler was tenacious concerning his lecturing; thus, he refused to sign the contract. Yet, the architectural sketch of the building that never materialized still hangs in Sadler's former office on Diversey Street.[63]

Dr. John Harvey Kellogg, who was interested in the Hull House social service center, founded in Chicago by Jane Addams, invited Sadler to work with this project; however, because Sadler felt that physical health could not be taught separate from spiritual health, their association never actualized.[64]

Sadler believed that the laity was passing through a period of popular reaction against the scientific materialism of the last century. "The common people are awaking to the fact that the mental state has much to do with bodily health and disease."[65]

We have reached that time in the awakening of the health consciousness of the American people when the man or woman of average intelligence is beginning to appreciate

---

[63] Sadler's Papers.
[64] Ibid.
[65] William S. Sadler, The Physiology of Faith and Fear or The Mind in Health and Disease (Chicago: A. C. McClurg & Co., 1912), p. vii. Hereafter cited as Sadler, Physiology of Faith and Fear.

the value of maintaining good health - and further, that health is usually better promoted by *doing* something than by *taking* something.[66]

Eventually Sadler gave surgery and entered into psychiatry full time. In 1911 he went to Europe to study under Freud. Although he respected Freud, he rejected his notion of fixed symbols.

> *Now, I don't mean by this that I am a believer in all the nonsense that has been put out under the guise of modern Freudian philosophy. When I have a patient who has a sex worry, I find the Freudian system very helpful in trying to get at the bottom of the thing and helping them over their trouble; but when it comes to the belief that all forms of worry, tension and nerves are of a sex origin, then I dissent. While we all recognize much that is valuable in Freud's teaching, it should be stated that he has not convinced the majority of psychologists and psychotherapists that all nervous disorders have a sex origin.*
>
> *We recognize that there are other human instincts and impulses just as strong as the sex urge. First of all there comes the instinct to live, to get food, and then, in many individuals, the religious emotion is very powerful, so that we cannot accept the Freudian doctrine that all our nervous troubles are due to suppression of the emotions and further that the particular emotion suppressed that is responsible for the trouble is the sex emotion.*[67]

Sadler found some of the quotations from ancient philosophers an assistance to his nervous patients. He suggested

---

[66] William S. Sadler, *The Chicago Therapeutic Institute: The Reliance Baths* (Chicago: Press of Winship Co., 1916), p. 29.
[67] Sadler, *Americznitis*, pp. 36 - 37.

that the worrier should often read this quote from Marcus Aurelius:

> *Do not disturb thyself by thinking of the whole of thy life. Let not thy thought at once embrace all the various troubles which thou mayest expect to befall thee; but on every occasion ask thyself, "What is there in this which is intolerable and past bearing?" ... remember that neither the future nor the past claims thee, but only the present....* [68]

Sadler agreed with the old physician, Rhazes; dyadic communication did have power in bringing about the cure of some patients. Rhazes believed that many illnesses were psychological:

> *In the 9th century, the great physician Rhazes attended an emir who was so badly crippled that he could not walk. First Rhazes ordered the emir's best horse to be saddled and brought into the court-yard. Rhazes gave the emir hot showers and a stiff drink. Then, brandishing a knife, he cursed his patient, threatened to kill him. Furious, the crippled man sprang to his feet. With his patient hot on his trail, the doctor leaped on the horse and escaped.* [69]

According to his close associates, Sadler maintained a schedule of perpetual activity; assiduously devoting himself to his practice, to his lecturing, and to his prolific writing. Only by diligent attention to essentials, promptness in dealing with details and selective apportionment of energy was he able to carry out these demanding undertakings. "Perhaps there are a few minutes between acts when he sits

---

[68] William S. Sadler, *Practice of Psychiatry* (St. Louis: The. C. V. Mosby Company, 1953), p. 907. Hereafter cited as Sadler, *Psychiatry*.
[69] "Wolf Broth for Arthritis," *Time*, November 25, 1940, p. 71.

down to dictate letters or write another chapter of the book. Always loaded to the limit and beyond..."[70]

Before the age of forty, he stayed up all night during one night of each week and dictated to two secretaries. He had a remarkable memory. While dictating books he mentioned that words just flowed before eyes as though on a movie screen.[71] His personal secretary of seventeen years mentioned that the notes that he took concerning his patient's diagnosis were meager; yet, after several years had elapsed, she could pull a case history from the file and he would fill in the details. In spite of these heavy demands, Sadler remained a "cheerful, optimistic man" because his joy was in his work which was basically interacting with people.[72]

As a psychiatrist, he worked with mentally disturbed and nervous patients. He was prompt in keeping his appointments with them, and he took time to describe their prognosis in simple terms. "He had a tremendous capacity for listening to his patients;"[73] and he would often console them by saying:

> *No use to worry -- worry ruins your mind. Worry is like paying interest on a loan at the bank -- on money you've never borrowed. If you can do something about a situation do it, if you can't just adjust to it. ... Do not be fearful of life; the universe is friendly.*[74]

---

[70] "The Message of Health For the Masses," *The Lyceumite and Talent*, III, No. 10 (March, 1910), 33. Hereafter cited as "Message For the Masses."

[71] Rawson Interview.

[72] Rawson Interview.

[73] Ibid.

[74] Christy Interview.

Sadler's students were advised, "Don't forget semantics. A word may mean one thing to the doctor and something entirely different to the patient."[75] Revealing his concern for his patients, he often remarked, "There is nothing wrong with them; they have just decided to be invalids, and their mind is playing a trick on them."[76] One illustration of a successful technique which Sadler employed was related by his daughter. A patient would come into the doctor's office and would believe that his arm was paralyzed. After giving the patient a complete physical, and after ascertaining that it was the mind and inner thoughts that needed to be changed, he would set up electrical machinery and pretend it was especially designed for that patient. After informing the patient that he thought that he could cure him, he would prop up his pseudo - paralyzed arm and ostensibly give a few electric shots in the arm. Then he would gradually take the prop away and try to convince the patient that he was no longer paralyzed.[77]

Occasionally Sadler discovered insights into the workings of the human mind almost by accident, as in the case of a hypochondriac who more or less cured himself. He used this true experience illustration in his "Faith and Fear" lecture:

> *Into my clinic many years ago there came a colored man with some minor complaint. After placing a thermometer under his tongue, closing his lips with great care, asking him to breathe through his nose and keep his mouth closed, I left him seated in one corner of the room. In the meantime I continued my lecture and quite forgot about the patient. After some thirty minutes I chanced to glance about the*

---

[75] Sadler, *Psychiatry*, p.833
[76] Christy Interview.
[77] Christy Interview.

> room and discovered him sitting like a statue in the exact position I had left him. I immediately went over to him and, taking the thermometer out of his mouth, inquired, "Well, how are you feeling now?" Imagine my astonishment upon receiving this reply, "Well, professah, I didn't taste nothin' but I sho' do feel better." This colored gentleman undoubtedly had never seen a thermometer, and like the patient with the paralysis, supposed he had been receiving some new and mysterious treatment. At any rate, after three applications of the thermometer on alternate days, he declared himself to be sufficiently improved to resume work at his old job.[78]

In expressing himself freely with patients, Sadler instilled the trust factor; his patients sensed that nothing that they revealed ever shocked him. Patients had an adoration and respect for him. Although he was never unkind, he was frank in pointing out mistakes and seldom offered compliments. This was in accord with his philosophy that people can do a great deal in their own maintenance of health.[79]

> The genuine psychiatrist ... does not want to build up a constituency of semiworshipping weaklings who are ever dependent upon his advice and guidance. He should crave the fellowship of a great group of men and women who are so thoroughly cured of their neurotic tendencies as to be quite free from the necessity of depending upon him for continuous guidance....[80]

To the same end, Sadler devoted considerable effort to improve the public attitude toward scientific psychiatry and the dangers presented by the incompetents seeking profit

---

[78] William S. Sadler, *The Truth About Mind Cure* (Chicago: A. C. McClurg & Co., 1928), pp. 73 - 74. Hereafter cited as Sadler, *Mind Cure*.
[79] Rawson Interview.
[80] Sadler, *Psychiatry*, p. 845.

for treatment of emotional disorders. In a speech delivered to the American Psychiatric Association, Sadler urged upon his fellow practitioners a continual campaign to educate the public to the "increasing menace of pseudo - psychologists, ignorant mental - hygienists, and half - baked practitioners of psychiatry, to say nothing of the clairvoyants, soothsayers, and spiritualistic mediums."[81] He deplored the paucity of psychiatric information that was being offered in the medical schools, believing that all physicians ought to be "psychiatrically minded."[82] To demonstrate that this concern was more than academic, Sadler had established a private clinic for physicians in Chicago, where at no cost, accredited physicians could receive in a two year's course "65 hours of didactic and 65 hours of clinical work."[83] Dr. Sadler reported that, although "this clinic was started with many misgivings," the sessions were well attended by interested and appreciative students.[84]

Adherence to the ethical requirements of the American Medical Association generally signified the professional concern of the practicing physician; to ignore them was *prima - facie* evidence of questionable activities. The admonishment against advertising was a recurrent subject in official statements of the Association.

> *Solicitation of patients by physicians as individuals, or collectively in groups ... is unprofessional ... It is equally unprofessional to procure patients by ... indirect advertisement, or by furnishing or inspiring newspaper or magazine comments concerning*

---

[81] Sadler, "Psychiatric Educational Work," pp. 4 - 5.
[82] Ibid, p. 6.
[83] Sadler, "Psychiatric Educational Work," p. 9.
[84] Ibid, p. 10.

> cases in which the physician has been or is concerned.[85]

Consequently, in 1910, as was the practice of leading physicians in the city of Chicago, Sadler's name was not to be found on the door of his office.[86] This regard for propriety must have caused some difficulties for the type of services which Sadler wished to render. On the second floor of the building at 100 State Street was located the Chicago Institute of Physiologic Therapeutics, founded by Sadler in 1907. The purpose of this institution was to render diagnostic and surgical services, plus physical and psychological therapeutic assistance to patients who came "on the instruction of some reputable medical practitioner."[87]

Sadler described this clinic as "a thoroughly equipped and scientifically conducted institution ... where every modern diagnostic facility necessary for the thorough and complete examination of a patient ... could be administered under competent medical supervision, and in accordance with professional ethics."[88] He carefully stressed the efforts which were made to enter into complete cooperation with the referring physician. In keeping with the principles of medical ethics which frowned upon those physicians who "... would boast of cures and remedies [or would] ... employ any of the other methods of charlatans."[89] Sadler's references to the clinic could be described as modest and unassuming.

---

[85] *1846-1958 Digest of Official Actions*, American Medical Association, 1st ed. (1959), I, 670.
[86] "Message For the Masses," p. 33.
[87] "Message For the Masses," p. 33.
[88] Sadler, The Chicago Therapeutic Institute.
[89] Principles of Medical Ethics of the American Medical *Association* (Chicago: Medical Association Press, 1903).

Among the first pioneers to write for the popular press were Dr. Woods Hutchinson and Sadler. An associate editor of the *Ladies Home Journal* came to the Sadler clinic ostensibly for an examination in 1911. She informed them that the editor of the magazine would be coming to Chicago to ask him to write *for* his magazine. Merle Crowell, the editor, persuaded Sadler to write several articles concerning health. However, when later Sadler was asked to send pictures with the articles, he feared that this request would be labeled unethical by the American Medical Association.

> Since no Doctor had ever had his picture in a magazine or newspaper without losing his membership in the American Medical Association, it was necessary that the way be cleared for such an unprecedented move, before Mr. Crowell's request could be met. [90]

With determination mixed with doubt and a feeling of trepidation, he approached the American Medical Association and the American College of Surgeons to seek advice. Both associations agreed that it was time for the public to be instructed in the essentials of preventive medicine and personal hygiene. They gave him permission to submit the pictures and offered to back him in this test of the ethical code.

The *Index Medicus,* a quarterly classified record of the current medical literature of the world, lists Sadler's first article, "The Influence of the Oxygen Bath on Blood Pressure," as having been written for the medical profession in 1910. Four other articles, "Curing Sick People Without Medicine," "Can We Really Stop Worrying," "What Wears

---

[90] Sadler's Papers.

Thousands of Us Out," and "Making a Child What We Want Him to Be," were written for the lay readers in the *Ladies Home Journal* the same year. During the years 1905 to 1926, only two other articles appeared in a Medical journal: "The Practice of Preventive Medicine," and "The Treatment of Intestinal Stasis"; however, many were written for the popular press. The subjects that he wrote about were outgrowths of his lectures. These articles bore such titles as: "Ways to Work Out Your Own Mind Cure," "Are You Committing Suicide On the Installment Plan?" "Cause and Cure of Colds," "Don't Fool With Tonics, They May Fool You," "Lost Your Pep?" "Stop Coddling Yourself," "They're Your Feet But Stop Abusing Them," "What To Do at Your Age to Protect Your Health," "What You Can Do About Your Heredity," "How the Mind Causes and Cures Disease," "We're All Afraid of Something," "College Women and Race Suicide," "Why We Get Fat and What To Do About It," and "Juvenile Manic Activity." He wrote one article for the *Journal of Criminal Law* on "Sterilization of the Unfit."[91] "Suburban and the City Child," evolved from his Chautauqua lecture dealing with health conditions in the city slums. This list of titles is not exhaustive; however, the titles of many of his other articles are listed in the bibliography.

In addition to such articles, Sadler was the author of forty

---

[91] The writer attempted to obtain some indication of the popularity of Sadler's books by contacting the publishing houses involved. Such specific information was not available; however, the General Sales Manager of C. V. Mosby Company offered the comment, "I do know from conversation with some of the older members of the firm that Dr. Sadler's books were among the brighter lights on the publishing horizon." Based on personal correspondence between Terry H. Green, General Sales Manager of the C. V. Mosby Company, and the writer, February 18, 1970.

- two books, many of which were outgrowths of his lectures.⁴⁹ In the following pages brief resumes of these books which reflect the direction of his oratorical efforts will be given. These are presented at this time on the supposition that they will reveal the nature of his concerns.

Only nine of his forty - two books will be reviewed, as they were results of his Chautauqua lectures. He had lectured on "Americanitis" for twenty years before making the speech extant in book form. Its basic thesis revealed that heredity and modern high tension was the cause of toxic tension, nervous tension and blood - pressure tension. A few book reviews in 1925 noted with some asperity:

> Dr. Sadler covers the ground adequately; his discussion of toxic Tension, Nervous Tension and Blood Pressure Tension is couched in terms intelligible to laymen and is yet sound scientifically. The tone of the book is injured somewhat by the jocosities of the author who writes a good deal like a Chautauqua lecturer addressing a hot - weather audience of weary morons.⁹²

> *Americanitis, as a disease entity, is not very clearly established by the book, but this is a minor detail for it is avowedly a piece of popular writing. Dr. Sadler rambles through his subject like a preoccupied professor in springtime who has his hour to fill but has left his notes at home. However, he gives throughout his frank opinion on matters which are vital, and he registers very definite protests against our habits of unhealthful thinking and the vices of unhygienic living.*⁹³

---

⁹² Marion A. Knight and Mertice N. James (eds.), *The Book Review Digest*, XXI (New York: H. W. Wilson Co., 1926), 617.

⁹³ *New York Tribune*, September 20, 1925, p. 10; and *Outlook*, CXL (August 5, 1925), 501.

"Men and Morals: A Lecture for Men Only," a regular offering on the Chautauqua circuit coupled with other lectures on health and Sadler's personal interest in salesmanship led to the creation of the popular lecture, "What Every Salesman Should Know About His Health," and the book which followed. An elaborate treatment of this lecture will appear in chapter five of this paper. His book, *The Physiology of Faith and Fear*, was an expansion of the following Chautauqua lectures: "Worry and Its Mental Cousins," "The Psychology of Faith and Fear," "The Physiology of Faith and Fear," "The Bible on Faith arid Fear," "The Humbugs of Healing," and "The Moral Management of Mental Maladies."[94] This book illustrated how the mind affects the body and how the fundamental mental states of faith and fear make for or against health. Theories were derived from actual experiments, clinical observations and laboratory investigations.

Worry and Nervousness, or the Science of Self-Mastery was an extension of his lecture, "The Cause and Cure of Worry or How to Banish the Blues." Sadler made a classification of seven sorts of nervousness, based on his own study of the cases that had come under his care. "Faith and Fear," a Chautauqua lecture, was written for publication under the title, *The Truth About Mind Cure*.

> Dr. Sadler, after twenty - five years of sympathetic study of the mind cure groups, now makes his report, giving the public the benefit of his long and varied experience ... Discussing it from a popular angle, yet keeping to the scientific facts, ...[95]

A lecture prepared for business women on mental, physical

---

[94] Sadler, *Physiology of Faith and Fear*.
[95] Sadler, *Mind Cure*, paper jacket.

and moral factors making for success later, emerged as a book entitled *Personality and Health*. *The Cause and Cure of Colds* discussed the causes of colds and the treatment of colds in their different stages.

> So many thousands suffer from common colds each year, so much time is lost by them, so much money expended on them, and there is such a weakening of vitality as a result of them that this Chautauqua lecture is now published ...[96]

During World War I, Sadler participated in an under cover organization of security and measures of a volunteer protective association. According to his daughter, this was extremely secretive, and nothing but the mention of the fact was revealed in his papers.[97]

Sadler believed that anthropology was the answer to the cause of the war. He not only lectured to the Chautauqua circuits concerning this, but at the request of the Secretary of State, he used the lecture for the nucleus of his book, *Long Heads and Round Heads*. In it he stated:

> Germany today is peopled by a docile, round - headed race with an inherited tendency to cruelty, viciousness, and with no more morals than a wolf. He claims they are Alpines, an inferior, stupid and non - progressive race, and are not real Teutons, having nothing whatever in common with that long - headed progressive and intelligent race.[98]

---

[96] *The Book Review Digest*, VI, No. 12, January - December (Minneapolis, Minnesota: H. W. Wilson Co.), 347.
[97] Christy Interview.
[98] W.S. Sadler, *Long Heads and Round Heads or What's the Matter with Germany* (Chicago: A. C. McClurg & Co., 1918), paper jacket. Hereafter cited as Sadler, *Long Heads and Round Heads*.

In 1911, Sadler began giving public addresses concerning spiritualism. He had had many patients under his professional care who had been clairvoyants, mediums, trance talkers, psychics, and sensitives. Due to the great interest factor pertaining to spiritualism following the war, A. C. McClurg and Company, his publishers, asked Sadler to prepare the transcript of his lecture for publication.[99]

Sadler had an unusual interest in the spiritualism phenomenon. At one time he worked with Howard Thurston, the magician, in the exposure of frauds, fakes, and mediums in the Chicago area.[100]

It is not the intention of this paper to make the claim that Sadler was solely responsible for major changes in the American Medical Association or in the attitudes of the lay public toward medicine and medical practitioners. It may well be that such changes were forthcoming by the very nature of the social structure and dynamic institutions which were contributing to the evolutionary movement of American society. Certainly, in his own mind, and in the opinions of many who knew him, he had had a role of more than average significance. That change was occurring is attested to in statements found in the *Index and Digest of Official Actions,* published by the American Medical Association, where a record of a 1914 report mentions:

> *Of late years the American Medical Association, through its Council on Health and Public Instruction has endeavored to spread broadcast knowledge of*

---

[99] William S. Sadler, *The Truth About Spiritualism* (Chicago: A. McClurg & Co., 1923), p. v.
[100] Sprunger Interview.

> *preventive medicine and public hygiene. It has endeavored to educate the public to an appreciation of what physicians and surgeons are doing and what are their aims and ideals in medicine. This has aroused a widespread interest in the public mind, and the public press has eagerly seized on this propaganda as news which interests its readers and which is, therefore, something to be sought and published. This has been legitimate work of public benefit and for the public good, and no one questions that it should be highly commended.*
>
> *Certain newspapers have heralded this stepping over the limits of the former strict adherence of the profession to its non-advertising principles as something laudatory and much to be desired.*[101]
>
> Although this change had taken place, the American Medical Association was still persistent in its efforts to prevent the abuse which this new freedom could possibly give birth to.[102]

Sadler's position followed the logic that people were going to get their information from other sources less authentic and reliable; therefore, it was the responsibility of capable authorities to provide them with the correct inclination:

> *...I myself am tempted to feel that it might be better to shut up like a clam and make an end of all this effort to instruct the layman, but my better judgment admonishes me that this is not the solution of the problem. Whether it pertains to science, philosophy, or religion, if a little knowledge is dangerous and the public already has this deleterious minimum of information, then there is but one solution of the problem - competent teachers must step into the*

---

[101] *Index and Digest of Official Actions: American Medical Association Beginning with the Year 1904* (Chicago: American Medical Association, 1942), p. 128. Hereafter cited as *Index and Digest of Official Actions*.
[102] Ibid. pp. 128 - 130.

> *picture and give the layman sufficient authentic information to take the danger out of the little knowledge he has.*[103]

When Sadler entered the practice of psychiatry full time, he did not abdicate his self - chosen mission of health instruction and preventive medicine. Rather, he believed that the mental - hygiene movement could profit and learn from the earlier experience "gained in the propagation of preventive medicine."[104] Consistent with his efforts to educate the public concerning physical hygiene, he began a public educational program concerning mental hygiene; he urged his fellow psychiatrists to "make every possible effort to remove from the public minds the stigma attached to mental, emotional, and personality disorders."[105] He attacked quackery in mental medicine and strategically sought to provide enlightenment about mental problems to those individuals whose relationship with the public were most apt to bring them into contact with victims of such disorders.

Following the pattern of his classes in psychiatry for physicians, Sadler initiated a clinic for similar instruction of ministers, priests and rabbis. This "pastoral psychiatry clinic [was] designed to help a minister of religion to a better understanding of the psychic, emotional, and personality problems of those who seek his counsel."[106] The carefully designated purpose of this instruction was to help ministers become personal counselors and to know when the services of trained psychiatrists were necessary.

Sadler found opportunity to expand this teaching work

---

[103] Sadler, "Psychiatric Educational Work," p. 14
[104] Ibid, p. 29.
[105] Ibid.
[106] Ibid, p. 23.

even further when the president of McCormick Theological Seminary, Dr. John Timothy Stone, asked him to direct a course in pastoral psychiatry for theological students of the seminary. Dr. Sadler began this teaching task in 1930 and continued as a professorial lecturer until 1955.[107] Later Sadler was to recall this experience as "one of the most rewarding and stimulating in a long and exciting career."[108]

The theological students taking this course were instructed:

> ... in the art of becoming better ministers of mental hygiene ... what cases they may safely undertake to help; how they may cooperate with the family physician, on the one hand, and with the psychiatric specialist, on the other; and ... what cases not to undertake.[109]

It is apparent that the medical and psychiatric career of Sadler afforded many and varied opportunities for public speaking. It is also apparent that he enjoyed this aspect of his active career.[110] It might be concluded that he had a natural talent and affection for the speaker's platform. However, as has been indicated earlier in this paper, Sadler's youthful ventures in oratory had benefited by pragmatic encouragement; he, himself, had pursued the study of rhetoric while in college.

---

[107] Based on personal correspondence between-the Office of-the president of McCormick Theological Seminary, and the writer, January 7, 1970.
[108] Sadler's Papers.
[109] Sadler, "Psychiatric Educational Work," pp. 24 - 25.
[110] William S. Sadler, *What A Salesman Should Know About His Health* (3d ed.; Chicago: The Dartnell Corporation, 1926), p. 110. Hereafter cited as Sadler, *Salesman*.

Significantly, the lecturing career of young Sadler was not begun without some personal concern and introspection. As a result, he sought the professional guidance of a professor of speech at the University of Chicago shortly after his decision to engage in public address. On several occasions he told the story of how this lady professor had him lecture to her; afterwards she said:

> Get out of here. I can't teach you anything. You're very bad; your gestures are atrocious. But you are so effective I wouldn't change anything about you; I'll ruin you if I change you.[111]

Years later this same speech professor happened to be in one of his audiences. She came up to the platform after he had finished speaking and uttered to Sadler, "You're just as bad as ever, but so damn effective. You can just hold an audience spellbound; I'm so glad that we didn't change you."[112]

Since the writer had only one opportunity to view Sadler in a speaking situation, she sent one hundred forty - six questionnaires to his former students from the McCormick Theological Seminary to learn their interpretation of the dynamics of his delivery.[113]

---

[111] Christy Interview

[112] Ibid.

[113] *Pronunciatio* [delivery] was a canon that held the utmost importance in the art of persuasion as theorized by the ancient rhetoricians. Cicero alluded to this fact as he wrote, "Delivery, I assert, is the dominant factor in oratory; without delivery the best speaker cannot be of any account at all,..."; E. W. Sutton and H. Rackham (trans.), *Cicero De Oratore* (Cambridge: Harvard University Press, 1942), III. lvi. 213. Hereafter cited as *Cicero De Oratore*. He believed that "by action the body talks"; Ibid, III. lix. 222. and "... delivery is wholly the concern of the feelings, and these are mirrored by the face and

The class rosters of the students were obtained from Sadler's personal papers. Only students from his lists, beginning with the year 1951 and ending with the year 1954, were selected; the ones whose current addresses were easily accessible were used. Sixteen to nineteen years had elapsed since the students had sat in Sadler's classes. Most of the students had retained the notes from his lectures; the writer was pleasantly amazed that his students could elicit such detailed descriptions after so many years. One of his former students, Wayne Benson, could not remember much about Sadler's gesticulations, but he sent a sketch he had drawn in his class revealing Sadler lecturing with his hands in his pockets. George F. Bennett, a student in the fall of 1954, wrote:

> *Dr. Sadler appeared quite elderly, rotund, with thick white hair (almost silver), thick, gold - rimmed glasses, a heavy-jowled face, almost always wearing a gray suit, starched white shirt, and slightly behind - the - times tie. He walked toward the lectern with short quick strides, spoke in a strong yet soft voice, started lecturing from his manuscript but quickly drifted from it to give almost two hours of lively anecdotes, almost all funny, and only on one or two occasions touching on anything "off color." He moved about freely, never consulted his manuscript after starting to lecture, gave the appearance of maintaining constant eye - contact, and usually dismissed the class a moment or two before the final bell rang. His gestures must have been appropriate since I do not recall them but I do recall a lot of movement. His speed of delivery and general effect was something like a funny Walter Cronkite might be ... He said he had a "senile" tendency to repeat*

---

expressed by the eyes."; Ibid, III. lviii. 221. Cicero reiterated that "everything depends on the countenance, while the countenance itself is entirely dominated by the eyes." ; Ibid.

> *himself and asked that we interrupt him when this happened.*

Dr. Sadler's sense of humor, self-confidence, enthusiasm, and overall personality were above average.[114]

Student Charles Filson recalls his prof. as having:

> *... a delightful sense of humor, but a failing memory for things that happened in the immediate present. For example, he often told the same story two or three times ... but he was such a good story teller that it was funny even the third time around. His stories were usually quite relevant and beautifully illustrated whatever point he was trying to make. His confidence and enthusiasm for his subject gave him an almost youthful bravado.*[115]

Charles F. LaRue, from his 1956 class, wrote:

> *Dr. Sadler enjoyed meeting his McCormick classes. There could be no doubt in that. He lectured and laughed and we all laughed with him. He gave a very positive and (maybe) too optimistic impression about the success of psychiatry. We all laughed because his textbook was so expensive.*[116]

Donald H. Frank remarked that he had a fond memory of Dr. Sadler:

---

[114] Based on personal correspondence between Chaplain George F. Bennett, Department of Mental Health, Central State Hospital, and the writer, May 8, 1970.

[115] Based on information in a questionnaire to the writer from Charles Filson, Springfield, Illinois.

[116] Based on personal correspondence between Charles F. LaRue, KcKinney, Texas, and the writer.

> *He rarely used lecture notes although he referred to his book, Practice of Psychiatry. While he wasn't a great orator, he had an interesting style of delivery which kept his students hanging on to his words. I did not want to miss any of his lectures. I thought that he had a fantastic sense of humor which had his classes quickly put at ease. He enjoyed his subject immensely and shared his enthusiasm with us.[117]*

"I have enjoyed thinking back to Dr. Sadler's course and the opportunity of putting down some of my reflections," was written in a letter by former student, C. Daniel Little. He continued to state:

> *Dr. Sadler's age, hairstyle, baggy dress, relaxed style and appearance, and his thorough involvement in his subject matter and his own approach to it, all went together to make for effective communication and easy listening.*
>
> *There were also aspects of his voice pattern and gestures which lent themselves to mimicry. Good laughs were had by a number of us back at the dorm as we imitated and appropriated his style.*
>
> *I would score Dr. Sadler especially high in sense of humor, self - confidence, and enthusiasm for his subject ... I can't say that I still use the material of the course, but I have no doubt that I continue to be influenced by the human approach of the man.[118]*

S. William Lankton remembered Sadler as a warm person with a good sense of humor who talked with authority.

---

[117] Based on personal correspondence between Donald H. Frank, Santa Anna, California, and the writer.

[118] Based on information in. a questionnaire to the writer from G. Daniel Little, New York, New York.

"Many times after that I used a number of his insights in sermons (with hardly the same sense of authority, though)." He related one interesting occurrence:

> *After graduation from seminary in June 1954, I was ordained & installed in a very small mission church in western Wyoming. During remodeling efforts on the church building I climbed under the building into a crawl - space and brought out an old pile of magazines. In one of them (I think from the 30's) was an article written by Dr. Sadler with his picture.*[119]

Donald E. Schomacker recalled "Dr. Sadler as being a peripatetic lecturer moving freely from the lectern much of the time."

> *He was not condescending to ministerial students as some physicians or experts in other fields might be but conveyed to us a sense that we might genuinely be helpful to persons who were emotionally distressed.*
>
> *The sense of humor was good and he was capable of sharing a joke, the butt of which was himself, upon occasion. He could relate events from the pioneering days of the Vienna school and his role there without seeming to dwell unduly on the past...*[120]

"He could be quite dramatic, even very outspoken, but never at a loss for words," wrote Albert G. Ossentjuk.

> *I recall references, quips, ways of saying things etc. that made the course quite interesting for me both*

---

[119] Based on information in a questionnaire to the writer from G. William Lankton, Chicago, Illinois.

[120] Based on information in a questionnaire to the writer from Donald E. Schomacker, Kansas City, Missouri.

> *academically and toward better self - understanding. I suppose that what I appreciated most was the awareness of individual humanity and Dr. Sadler's readiness to take a person as he is.* [121]

Murray Travis remembered Sadler as "an engaging lecturer. He maintained good eye contact, was fairly free of the lectern ... and made adequate use of gestures."

> *He had a good sense of humor and could tell some delightful stories of patients and experiences. He possessed self-confidence and had great enthusiasm for his subject; his concern for his subject was reflected in his life and the pioneering he had done in the field. This same concern and enthusiasm was reflected in his teaching.* [122]

"He had the attention of the students all the way. I still recall his quote about the spite fence built by a paranoid; I think it was about 20 feet high. It is not funny except when you have heard him tell of it," wrote Sadler's former student, Richard H. Burgess. Burgess mentioned that Sadler's influence is still present:

> *I recall his teaching on systematizing your work. He taught a boy who was so sloppy that his parents couldn't stand it taught the boy to take care of tasks immediately.... (This precept I am following in immediately filling in this questionnaire.) ... More of this speaking from experience is needed in our universities, less of the pure theory approach.* [123]

---

[121] Based on information in a questionnaire to the writer from Albert G. Ossentjuk, Denver, Colorado.
[122] Based on information in a questionnaire from Murray Travis, Tulia, Texas.
[123] Based on information in a questionnaire from Richard H. Burgess, Poynette, Wisconsin.

Almost all of the students mentioned Sadler's sense of humor and his contagious enthusiasm for his subject matter. Calvin Didier not only mentioned his sense of humor but other aspects of his presentation:

> *It was the quality of his mind as expressed in what he said that seemed to be the whole magnetism of his presentation. He did make effective use of pause, sometimes even turning away from the class and looking out the window to the side. I suppose there was a natural drama in the way he presented a thought. But it seemed largely unconscious in that I never sensed he was "acting."* [124]

Student Charles Dierenfield reported that "I do not think that the years have blurred my memory of him...because I was very much taken with Dr. Sadler in his course and it was one of the better courses that we had in Seminary."

> *His clothes were of a more comfortable nature and gave you at all times the complete impression of self possession. He knew exactly what he was doing; that he knew who he was, and was perfectly satisfied with the result. He was not "up tight" at any time.*
>
> *I felt that while he had a quiet personality, he was an extremely dynamic man. It was like a 16 cylinder idling; we knew that there was a lot there if he ever wanted to apply it and so it gave a vitality and a quality to his lectures and relationships.* [125]

Lawrence Woodcock especially remembered that "his description of his time with Freud and Adler, and his

---

[124] Based on information in a questionnaire from Calvin Didier, Detroit Michigan.
[125] Based on information in a questionnaire from Charles Dierenfield, Newport Beach, California.

differences with them, was impressive.[126]

"My attitude toward Dr. Sadler was that he must have been quite a professional in his day." Even though it had been fifteen years since Morgan S. Roberts studied under Dr. Sadler, he reflected that:

> *I never remember him sitting at a desk or even using a lectern. His entire lecture was given standing up, pacing back and forth across the front of the room. His voice was rather high pitched but he had good inflections. A good percentage of his lectures were recounting of experiences and he could become quite wrapped up in some of them.*[127]

The Reverend John W. Omerod remembered that:

> ... he was a forceful speaker in the classroom ... Each student had the feeling that he was speaking directly to him because of his constant eye contact with each person. Dr. Sadler was so attuned to the class that he sensed when someone missed the point he was making; and often, by the use of gestures would restate his point effectively. By the quality and timbre of voice, he could place a parenthetical statement in a sentence and students would know that it was parenthetical.[128]

It was difficult for John R. Dilley to categorize Dr. Sadler as a personality: "At times, he impressed me as a jolly little old man whom you would like your children to know.

---

[126] Based on information in a questionnaire from Lawrence Woodcock, Blackwell, Oklahoma.

[127] Based on information in a questionnaire from Morgan S. Roberts, Portland, Indiana.

[128] Based on information in a questionnaire from The Reverend John W. Omerod, Toronto, Ohio.

Other times, he would come on as a shrewd business tycoon ... "However, Mr. Dilley vividly remembered Sadler's presentation:

> He had tremendous audience contact, and was concerned that everyone was following him. He moved about rather extensively as he lectured, sitting on the corner of a table ... or balancing on the back of a chair.
>
> He always had stories to share ... he would have referred to them as "case histories." These stories would just flow from him, one after the other. Very seldom did he refer to notes, and very seldom did he refer to other authors or sources other than himself.
>
> His sense - of - humor almost always took on the tone of a person being humiliating ... to him, this humiliation was a form of humor.[129]

"I recall his manner of delivery as a kind of sharing session that had the captivating quality of respect for us, his students, whom he chose to include as equals, thinking with us, never talking down to us," wrote Ronald T. Allin, who had been away from Sadler's classroom for nineteen years.

> I recall ... the intensity of eye contact, and the remarkable ability he had to give every student in his class, at least for me, the feeling of talking personally and directly with me. He moved around a lot, a kind of peripatetic conversation more than a formal lecture. His tone of voice and quality of speaking simply do not recall as significant. It was so effective in communicating, that I was simply unaware of tone quality and characteristics of speaking voice. This

---

[129] Based on information in a questionnaire from John R. Dilley, Fairfield, Iowa.

> *may be the highest compliment one can pay a speaker. His delivery was at times slow and thoughtful and at others rapid and animated. The speaking style depended upon the content and was completely complimentary to it. I recall his use of the black board as rather impressionistic in that the diagrams were symbolic rather than accurate and the key words were effectively listed.*[130]

Robert E. Raymond replied, "Chiefly I remember his humor his illustrations always made the point hilariously clear." He remembered that Sadler always said, "You may not remember my lectures, but you will remember my stories."

> *And of course he was right -- I still (after 16 years) remember his stories -- and thus the material they related to. He had a clear, penetrating voice, looked like an Alfred Hitchcock. He had a John Kennedy sort of gesture with his index finger with which he punctuated his main points.*[131]

According to the eighty - eight questionnaires returned, all students mentioned the following points: Sadler's keen sense of humor[132] in relation to the case studies, his enthusiasm for his subject matter and his teaching, the illustrative

---

[130] Based on information in a questionnaire from Ronald T. Aiin, Chagrin Falls, Ohio.

[131] Based on information in a questionnaire front Robert E. Raymond, Waukesha, Wisconsin.

[132] Students, associates and relatives all attest to his humor. In an interview with his daughter-in-law, Leone, it was revealed that he even joked with strangers. "Dr. Sadler when speaking in Detroit was traveling on a street car to his lecture engagement. The man riding next to him asked him where he was going. When hearing the name of the hail, the passenger said, 'Oh, so you are going to hear Sadler speak - what do you think of him?' Sadler retorted, 'Why I wouldn't walk across the street to hear him speak.' When Sadler was introduced on

64

material that caused his lectures to live, and his total self - confidence.

On the questionnaire the writer asked for negative criticism. The overall return was that although Sadler was a warm, intimate person while lecturing, he was distant in dyadic conversation:

> *As I recall, Dr. Sadler ... didn't seem to have any particular interest in any particular student of the class I was in. This of course doesn't mean he wasn't interested in his students as a class.*[133]

In a letter received from Charles Dierenfield, he stated:

> *Thank you for the opportunity to speak about my friend, Dr. Sadler. I use the word 'friend' generally because it was mostly a teacher-student relationship, but I thought he was an outstanding man.*[134]

Rev. G. William Lankton related:

> *I didn't know him personally - it was one of those I-knew-him-but-he-didn't-know-me things. I did have a real affection for him during the time of the class, but never had any contact with him afterwards.*[135]

After sixteen to nineteen years the students were still aware

---

the platform that night, the fellow passenger who was then in the audience laughed throughout most of his lecture." Statement by Leone Sadler, personal interview, December 29, 1969.

[133] 91Based on information in a questionnaire from Robert L. Cobb, Salt Lake City, Utah.

[134] 92Based on personal correspondence between Charles Dierenfield, and the writer, May 14, 1970.

[135] Based on information in a questionnaire from Rev. C. William Lankton, Chicago, Illinois.

of Sadler's isolation of them as individuals:

> *I always felt, however, that he was at some distance from the individual student, having an enthusiasm for people in general rather than for students (at least this particular student) in particular.*[136]

Student George F. Bennett wrote about this distance in Sadler's interpersonal conversation:

> *He seemed to have a lack of interest in individual students ... and he responded briefly, appropriately, but with sufficient distance to ward off any attempt to establish a dependency or encourage fantasies of a "special relationship." I suspect that he made it a practice not to be "familiar" with strangers which is one of the few Victorian "virtues" that people who work with hospital or church populations probably need to develop.*[137]

"I had the feeling that Dr. Sadler's interest in student was much more general than particular," disclosed Calvin Didier in his negative criticism.

> *When I spoke to him about his method of marking, he was quite open in letting us know that he didn't know one student from another and could hardly care less about that. I came away with the feeling that he had just known too many people through too many years to care any more and was quite defensive about his time.*[138]

---

[136] Based on information in a questionnaire from G. Daniel Little, New York, New York.

[137] Based on information in a questionnaire from George F. Bennett, Louisville, Kentucky.

[138] Based on information in a questionnaire from Calvin W. Didier, Detroit, Michigan.

The criticism that his students presented corresponds with the information that was received from his daughter, Christy; his personal secretary of seventeen years; and his daughter - in - law, Leone. Sadler was a dynamic, demonstrative, extrovert on the platform, but otherwise had introvertive tendencies and did not care to fraternize or engage in talk of a trivial nature with individuals. He often related to his daughter that, "I am not a small talker -- I do not do well at cocktail parties -- those things bore me. But if I have an audience and somebody punches me in the right place, I'll start going just like a record."[139] Sadler referred to himself as an ambivert.

Sadler was no ordinary man or he could not have endured the pace in which he lived. Not only was he a surgeon and a psychiatrist, but he was a professor at the Post graduate medical school of Chicago, professor of pastoral Psychiatry, at McCormick Theological Seminary, and a staff member of Columbus Hospital. He held memberships in the following associations: Life Fellow American College of Surgeons, Fellow of the American Association for the Advancement of Science, Fellow of the American Medical Association, Fellow of the American Psychiatric Association, Member of American Psycho - Pathological Association, Member of Illinois Psychiatric Association, The Chicago Society for Personality Study, The Chicago Medical Society, The Illinois State Medical Society, Board Member, W. K. Kellogg Foundation, Battle Creek, The Eugene Field Society, International Mark Twain Society, National Association of Authors and Journalists, Founder Member, Gorgas Memorial Institute in Tropical and Preventive Medicine, and member of its governing board.

---

[139] Christy Interview.

Involvement in these institutions and their activities undoubtedly required effort; however, Sadler had a desire to extend his talents to the Lyceum and Chautauqua platform.

The Lyceum and Chautauqua platform appeared to be a very important part of Sadler's life. On January 1, 1911, in a letter to Harry P. Harrison, he wrote:

> *I am anxious to arrange for a conference with you as soon as possible with reference to the I.L.A. convention program. If we could arrange to have a meeting and carefully go over some matters ... I could start the ball a rolling. It would be an accommodation to me if I could see you sometime at 2:00, following office hours, or I could come in the city some morning that we did not have operations, early, if it will be more convenient to you, and in this event we would have a conference before my office hours ...*[140]

In 1911, after some of the barriers concerning advertising were relinquished by the Medical Association, Sadler became chairman of the International Lyceum Association Program Committee. He again reveals his strength in organization of professionalism, as he writes to Harry P. Harrison:

> *I find that W.N. Ferris of Big Rapids, Michigan, is not a member of the I.L.A. Would you feel free to write and invite him to attend the next convention and participate in the program on Committeemen's Day, and incidentally give him a strong invitation to join the I.L.A.? ... I also find that Rev. T. C. Pollock of*

---

[140] Based on personal correspondence between William S. Sadler and Harry P. Harrison, January 1, 1911.

> *Monmouth, Illinois, is not a member; but I have written him, asking him to join.* [141]

The Lyceum managers were proud to have a man of Sadler's caliber working for their platform. In an article in 1910, they stated that here was a lecturer who wanted to serve humanity and "to do good, not to get money, for it is evident that specialists and surgeons of this sort lose money every day they leave their work.[142] He welcomed opportunities to speak on their program. One Thursday morning at eleven o'clock Sadler lectured to an unusually large audience on "When Doctors Disagree." This was not one of Dr. Sadler's regular lectures, but was a special address prepared for the I.L.A. [International Lyceum Association] Chautauqua.

> *Dr. Sadler, it may be said, in taking to the platform, where he had won signal success as a lecturer, did so that he might the better work out a vision that came to him as a young man just out of college, that is, to educate the people to medical truths worthy of scientific propaganda. In his lecture Dr. Sadler dealt with questions close to the heart of every human being.* [143]

Dr. William S. Sadler, M.D., died on April 26, 1969, just three months before reaching the age of ninety-four. He was active until the end of his life, still doctoring a select group of patients until six months before his death. In the notice of his obituary, *The American Medical News* noted that

---

[141] Based on personal correspondence between William S. Sadler and Harry P. Harrison, Feb14, 1911.

[142] "Message For the Masses," p. 33.

[143] Speech given at the 1912 International Lyceum Association Convention, Winona Lake, Indiana, September 6. *The Lyceum News*, II, No. 8, September, 1912, pp. 8 - 10.

"in 1917, Dr. Sadler predicted that human organ transplants would be successfully performed and accepted by the public." [144]

> Dr. Sadler told the Wednesday club in East St. Louis on January 3, 1917, that the time was "not far distant when wealthy people will take mortgages on internal organs of healthy persons and have the organs transplanted into their bodies at the death of the mortgagor."[145]

His daughter, Christy, commented that at the eve of Dr. Sadler's life on earth his mind remained clear, logical and happy as he gave this final farewell to his loved ones:

> The transition from this world to the next is very easy. There is no pain. It is easy to leave the pains of this world for the pleasures of the next, and I am going to enjoy every moment of it. I am very conscious of everything that is going on here tonight. I could go on visiting with you for hours but it would be no use. The chapter is closed. The last lines have been written; the book is finished. This world is very real, but the next one is much more real.[146]

The purpose of this chapter has been to draw together several themes which have recurred throughout the life and career of William S. Sadler. From his early preparation and commitment there emerged an ability and a passionate dedication to a cause which filled his life with activity and persistent endeavor that was, to say the least, extraordinary. In review, it cannot be said that Sadler sought fame nor that he was famous. His purpose was to use his talents and

---

[144] "Medicine's Week in the Nation," *The AMA News:* The Newspaper of American Medicine, May 12, 1969, p. 1.
[145] "Sadler Obituary," *Chicago Tribune,* April 28, 1969, Sec.II, p.18.
[146] Christy Interview.

his training for the good of his fellow man. In carrying out this purpose he exemplified the classical definition of an orator – "a good man speaking well."

Since the study of oratory demands the examination of the orator, in order that his motives and his sincerity may be brought to light, the foregoing biographical material has been introduced. The writer believes that the evidence presents a positive case and that Sadler deserves to be included in the list of American orators who have, in one way or another, contributed to the rich cultural stream that flows through our society. In the following chapters, the nature of his contribution will receive specific analysis and comment. It will be seen that what he has done was an expression of the kind of person he was.

III. THE OCCASION

In rhetorical analysis, the occasion of a speech is in itself a matter of particular significance. A review of the period of American oratory in the nineteenth century and in the first quarter of the twentieth century cannot overlook the unique opportunities for oratory which were presented by the Chautauqua and Lyceum organizations. Documentation of the emergence and wide-spread diffusion of the Chautauqua platform supports the contention that this platform had great impact upon American institutions and especially upon rural and small-town Americans. In this study of the speaking career of William S. Sadler, because the Chautauqua platform was the occasion of his speaking, an examination of the organization and character of the Chautauqua seems to be a task of the critic.

Since speeches are products of their times and are prepared for specific occasions, it becomes the critics duty to discover how the speaker adapted and adjusted to the occasion of the speech. In the case of the Chautauqua such adaptation had to be qualified by the ethics of the platform, the physical setting, the composition of the audiences, and the immediate social and physical environment of the auditors. From the many records, reports, newspaper accounts, biographies, and personal files, a picture of the psychological and sociological setting can be filled in. Because the setting has an influence upon the style, organization, and manner of presentation of a speech, the following description of the occasion for Sadler's speaking will make a more complete analysis possible.

The term 'Chautauqua," except in American history books and in the memories of that dwindling segment of the population born around the turn of the century, arouses no excitement and little recognition today. That it was a dominant institution in American life for fifty years and touched the lives of more than thirty million American citizens and then passed into historical oblivion seems incredible. As will be shown in this chapter, the reason for Chautauqua's rise and fall lies in its identification with the specific needs of a people who were in a transition between the simple, agricultural, small - town life of the nineteenth century and the sophisticated, technologically complex urban life of the twentieth century. As the transition period continued, Chautauqua, and its unique contributions simply became a vestige of an age that had passed.

During its zenith, however, Chautauqua was hailed as the "peoples' university," the isolated community's salvation from provincialism, a vocal magazine in which truth was reinforced by personality.[147] It brought culture and education to a people stirring with the restless hunger of minds stimulated by social change and scientific advance. It gave the assurance that old verities would not be exchanged for new and irreverent extremes. At the same time, it may be conjectured, the Chautauqua enterprise may have planted the seeds of curiosity and self - actualization which eventuated in an accelerated demand for greater knowledge and worldly awareness.

The subject of this study, William S. Sadler, contributed to the history of Chautauqua, to its character and to its direction. Conversely, the style of life which *was* Chautauqua impressed itself upon his life and career. For that reason a further elaboration of Chautauqua appears justifiable.

---

[147] Edward Amherst Ott, "The Chautauqua Movement," *The Lyceumite and Talent,* XXIII (June., 1913), i.

At its beginning, the salient idea of the Chautauqua was to make more effective the impact of Christian influence upon a changing society. But by providing education for all classes of people, enlightenment for all grades of intellect, and common foci for branches of religion, the movement helped to bridge the chasm between classes of citizens. Through the Chautauqua movement, individuals had their cultural and inite1lectual horizons widened. Encouraged to read, stimulated to think, masses of Americans were ushered by it into the expanding worlds of literature, politics, health education, science, sociology and religion.[148]

The first Chautauqua in the world was launched in the summer of 1874 when a self - educated circuit - riding preacher, Bishop John H. Vincent, feeling thwarted in educational fields organized a group of people for the purpose of mental and moral improvement at Lake Chautauqua, New York. An associate, Lewis Miller, joined him in this venture.[149] This simple beginning took the name of a relatively unknown lake and caused it to reverberate into every city, town, and village in the United States. Thus, the word "Chautauqua" was changed from a picturesque Seneca Indian nomenclature to which authorities have assigned various meanings -- "where the fish was taken out," "the place of easy death," "the place where one was lost," "where the child was washed away," "a bag tied in the *middle*," "a pack *tied in the middle*," "*two*-moccasins - tied-in-the-middle," "a foggy place" - to a word synonymous with "culture."[150]

---

[148] Bishop John H. Vincent, "The Chautauqua," *The Lyceum Magazine* (July, 1910; November, 1910), on cover.

[149] *Through the Meshes* (Cleveland: W. C. Tyler Company, 1922). Hereafter cited as *Through the Meshes*.

[150] Louise Pound, "Miscellany: Chautauqua Notes," *American Speech*, IX, No. 3 (October, 1934), 233.

At that time adult education did not exist in America. The need to actualize intellectual and spiritual potentials gave impetus and direction to this first Chautauqua experiment. The founders had conceptualized the novel idea of a unified Sunday School course which would provide the Sunday School movement with educated teachers. Believing that Bible education could be made enjoyable and stimulating, Vincent and Miller developed teaching innovations which established patterns still followed in modern instruction. In these uncharted fields, they creatively organized courses, arranged subjects, and invented such devices as the model of Palestine, the Oriental House, and the Tabernacle in the Wilderness. There, beside the lake, Reverend Chautauquans gave lectures daily in mitre, robe and breast - plate in their efforts to bring life to the teaching of scriptual traditions.[151] "Chautauqua became synonymous with clean, wholesome, stimulating amusement, with educational features not to be found outside the walls of a college."[152]

During this era, colleges were sophisticated and aristocratic; they offered no summer sessions nor correspondence courses to satisfy a mental famine. People came in large numbers to hear Chautauqua speakers and to seek enrichment through its creative offerings. An intense loyalty, the "Chautauqua Spirit," was prompted by the institution and its leaders. Thousands who had the financial means came and through a tacit initiation were transformed into Chautauquans.[153]

---

[151] Elizabeth Vincent, "Old First Night," *The New Republic*, XL (September 24, 1924), 96.

[152] Ibid.

[153] *Some Chautauqua Facts*, Chautauqua Collections, The University of Iowa Chautauqua Collections (Chicago: Redpath Chautauquas), Msc - 150 Miscellaneous Programs. Hereafter cited as *Some Chautauqua Facts*.

The Chautauqua was destined for expansion. An earlier movement, the Lyceum, founded by Josiah Holbrook in 1826, was to participate in this expansion. Holbrook, a Connecticut educator, had originated the Lyceum idea when he organized a group of forty farmers and mechanics for the purpose of educational enlightenment.[154] The purpose of the group was suggested when Holbrook chose its name. Named after the Greek "Lyceum," an Athenian grove consecrated to Apollo whose surname was Lykeois, and made famous by Aristotle who taught philosophy there, the name conveyed the idea of teaching and learning which was what Holbrook had in mind.[155]

Ralph Waldo Emerson

In this first American lyceum, the more intelligent and learned members lectured to other members of the group. Eventually the group backlog of information was exhausted and it became expedient to invite other educated men to do the lecturing. Ralph Waldo Emerson was one of these early lecturers. He delivered ninety - eight lectures without charge; later his fee was five dollars, however, he soon stipulated that he had to have an extra "three quarts of oats for my horse."[156] Emerson's lecturing grew in popularity; he became in such demand that

---

[154] *Through the Meshes*, p. 14.
[155] Ralph M. Bradford, "The Value of Chautauqua," *The Billboard*, XXXVI (March 8, 1924), 1. Hereafter cited as Bradford, "Value of Chautauqua."
[156] Ibid.

he was eventually receiving five hundred dollars per lecture.[157]

Alexander Graham Bell in 1905

It was on February 14, 1877, in a Lyceum hail that Alexander Graham Bell delivered his first lecture about the telephone.[158] Other intellectual giants whose oratory lent distinction to the programs of the early Lyceum were: Henry Thoreau, James Russell Lowell, Daniel Webster, Oliver Wendell Holmes,[159] Wendell Phillips, Horace Greeley, Henry Ward Beecher, Mark Twain, and Henry James.[160]

During this early phase Lyceum speakers were engaged by direct negotiation with lecture committees. In 1868 James Redpath conceived the idea of making booking engagements for these popular men. In his proposals to these orators, Redpath suggested that he could not only save them voluminous correspondence but that he could obtain higher fees for their services. They were eager to join his bureau. To Redpath belongs the credit for initiating the management - agent concept and for instituting the bureau

---

[157] *Through the Meshe*s, p. 14.
[158] Bradford, "Value of Chautauqua," p. 1.
[159] Gregory Mason, "Putting the Talk in Chautauqua," *Outlook*, CXXVIII (July 6, 1921)~ 419. Hereafter cited as Mason, "Talk in Chautauqua."
[160] Bradford, "Value of Chautauqua," p. 1.

system by means of which all the lecture business of the country was subsequently conducted.[161] Some associates proposed that the Lyceum be operated for the benefit of charity. Redpath stated his opposition to this by saying, "Lyceum courses that are primarily run for charity generally fail within a year or two."[162]

James Redpath
[163]

Impressed by the successful Chautauqua Lake programs, inspired leaders established independent Chautauqua centers in other communities. Some were equally successful, while others suffered from lack of financial support caused mainly by poor planning and intense competition. These local Chautauquas provided programs and services, camping and recreation, the cost of which eliminated all but the well - to - do as clientele.[164]

The modern Lyceum movement founded by James Redpath soon motivated changes in the Chautauqua system. The Lyceum itself had started to move to the people by holding its meetings in buildings in various communities. With a demand for religious and educational opportunities

---

[161] *Some Chautauqua Facts*, p. 2.

[162] James Redpath, "The People's College," *Lyceum and Chautauqua*, XXV, No. 5 (October, 1915), cover.

[163] Thos. W. Herringshaw, *The Biographical Review of Prominent Men and Women of the Day*, (Chicago: Elliott and Beezley, 1889) 493.

[164] *Twenty Years of Chautauqua Progress: 1904 - 1923*, Chautauqua Collection (Cedar Rapids, Iowa: The Torch Press), p. 5, Msc - 150, Miscellaneous Programs. Hereafter cited as *Twenty Years of Progress: 1904-1923*.

in connection with summer recreational and social activities, the Chautauqua circuit was inevitable.[165] The Redpath Chautauqua system combined the manager - agent of the Lyceum and the varied programs of the original Chautauqua and established the circuiting Chautauqua. In 1908 The Redpath Lyceum and Chautauqua Bureau arranged a tour of one hundred towns, bringing the benefits of Chautauqua to the people in remote areas and providing the best talent possible.

The Redpath Chautauqua Special Enroute
from Chicago to Dixie Land, 1913

The proliferation of the circuit chautauqua in the Midwest may be attested by the fact that "in 1920 circuits serviced 436 communities in Iowa, 198 in Minnesota, 274 in Nebraska, 217 in Ohio, 260 in Kansas, 352 in Illinois, 208 in

---

[165] "The Evolution of the Chautauqua System," Editorial in *Journal of Education*, LXVIII, No. 8 (September 3, 1908), 1.

Wisconsin, 113 in Michigan and 164 in Indiana.[166]

Many other Chautauqua circuits burgeoned and tents were soon found in all parts of the United States, and by 1922, Canada had over five hundred Chautauquas. Australia and New Zealand also played host to the traveling Chautauquas and their canvas tents.[167]

Keith Vawter, manager of the Redpath-Vawter circuit, revealed these statistics in a speech to an advertising club:

> *Chairman of the Statistical Committee for the International Chautauqua Association in his report for 1920, reported the actual operation of 8,580 Chautauqua's with 5,757 employees. These figures indicate that the Chautauquas reached, in the summer of 1920, thirty - five million people. You will readily recognize that broadly speaking, a third of our population was reached by the Chautauqua's.*[168]

The mechanics of the organization of the circuit system were strategically systematic. It was the office of the superintendent or the office of a traveling agent of the bureau to secure a contract for the next year at the moment the Chautauqua was in town. Bureau managers informed their superintendents:

---

[166] William Cumberland, "A Classification of Circuit Chautauqua Programs and Talent for the Year 1924" (unpublished Master's thesis, State University of Iowa, 1963), p. 17.

[167] Joseph Devlin, "Lecturing While the Mercury Boils," *New York Tribune* (Sunday, August 19, 1923), p. 2, col. 4. Hereafter cited as Devlin, "Lecturing."

[168] Keith Vawter, Manager of the Redpath - Vawter Circuit in a Speech delivered to the Poor Richard (Advertising) Club, December 8, 1921, at Philadelphia, Pennsylvania, p. 5. Hereafter cited as Keith Vawter Speech.

> *Your work as Chautauqua superintendent will in most cases stand or fall by what you do in the contract situation.... It is assumed that you w11 succeed in every way in your Chautauqua work absolutely without a question. The only thing that the office is really interested in is whether or not you get contracts, because they take it for granted that the other parts of your work will be O.K.* [169]

Chautauqua managers promised the superintendents reinforcement in the form of a bonus if they secured the guarantors' signatures. They suggested techniques of obtaining these signatures in their handbook:

> *It is important that you go to work on your contract early. Get it signed up and in the mail before the closing day if you possibly can. We have never yet had a season when some superintendent did not report that the committee had promised to sign, but that a rain storm came up on the last night, and consequently he lost his contract. ... Go to your key man whom you should have spotted your first day in town and get him to start your contract.... After you get four or five leaders on your contract, it is generally easy to finish it around the gate at program times and on the street between programs.* [170]

The reinforcement theory was again used by the superintendents of equipment in order to receive the most efficient work from the property men. An exhaustive bulletin was sent to the property men describing in detail how to handle the canvas, ropes, chairs, poles, stage, wiring, lamps, trunks, pianos, etc. Threatened negative sanctions

---

[169] C. Benjamin Franklin, Handbook of Information and Instruction, Associated Chautauquas of America, No. 50, Redpath Collection, p. 28. Hereafter cited as Franklin, Handbook of Information.
[170] Ibid.

appeared in the bulletin:

> *I want all of you to know that I am the party who is mostly responsible for any deductions in bonuses. A badly loaded car or the failure of a Property Man to come direct to the Warehouse will, in a great measure tip me off as to what kind of care his equipment has received and will have a distinct bearing on the size of his as well as the entire crews bonuses.*[171]

The hardships and regimen that the Chautauqua personnel had to face took a certain degree of stamina. In the early part of the twentieth century a lecturer might have a contract to deliver ninety - one lectures in ninety - one days in ninety - one Middle Western towns.[172] Travel was not always comfortable; it was sometimes quite primitive. A new Chautauqua town must be reached each day, and often the towns were fifty or a hundred miles apart. Occasionally the Chautauqua tent would be pitched five or six miles from a town.[173] During storms the roads were sometimes in such bad condition that transfer companies refused to take the lecturers to the next town where their performance was being awaited.[174] It occasionally took three trains six or seven hours to reach a town forty or fifty miles distant.[175] Sometimes the talent found it necessary to ride on ancient

---

[171] Based on correspondence in a bulletin between Superintendent of Equipment and Warehouse, Ray Oster of Redpath Chautauqua. Copies sent to: 0. 0. Bottorf Property Men, Superintendents, Redpath Collection, Miscellaneous Collection, 150.

[172] Alma Ellerbe and Paul Ellerbe, "The Most American Thing in Ainerica,"The *World's Work*, XLVIII (1924), 440. Hereafter cited as Ellerbe and Ellerbe, "Most American Thing."

[173] "Lecturing," p. 2.

[174] Louise Treadwell, "Playing Chautauqua Stands," *The New York Times Magazine* (October 29, 1922), p. 3.

[175] Ibid.

patterned coaches hitched to freight trains, or on two - wheeled flat cars which were normally baggage carriers.[176] Trains were often late; thus, talent had to be resourceful in finding transportation to the next town in order to arrive in time for their scheduled spot on the program.

When there were no railroads available, Fords were utilized. One was fortunate to get a "flivver" which held together. When a lecturer had to ride twenty or thirty miles in a temperature of almost one hundred degrees over dusty roads which closely resembled cow paths, he suffered many bodily discomforts.[177] The physical tension and nervous strain was increased when one had to transfer from a car to a slow, smoke - filled train; one would sometimes reach his destination just in time for his performance without time to wash or eat. The managers expected their talent to have showmanship and to be impeccably dressed. This was problematic because the talent did not remain long enough at a hotel for the washing and drying of garments, and in many towns all business stores closed during Chautauqua week, thus causing the impossibility of getting clothes cleaned. There were inadequate conveniences, and during the summer when there was not enough water to wash hands and face, the talent was forced to seek a river or pond.[178]

Some small towns did not have hotels; when a farmhouse was not offered, the talent had to sleep on a plank bed in the tent.[32] Talent accepted these inconveniences for many reasons: some for money alone, others for political prominency, some for the thrill of performing in front of such

---

[176] Ibid., p. 4.
[177] Devlin, "Lecturing," p. 2
[178] Ibid

mass audiences, others for the love of serving humanity.

Letters of evidence lead the writer to believe that Sadler was a humanitarian in that he was not inspired by any monetary motive but in a sincere desire to serve mankind. Sadler wrote to Harry P. Harrison concerning lecturing on the winter Lyceum platform:

> It means a great deal to me to undertake to do Winter lecture work. ... I was thinking you might possibly have some calls for lectures about the city or its environs and which [sic] you might use me without money and without price.[179]

He believed as Hugh Blair, "Speech is the great instrument by which man becomes beneficial to man."[180] His decision to serve the laity, which was followed by sixty years of a prodigious labor of love and included the writing of numerous books and articles, inspired him to speak thousands of times to audiences totaling hundreds of thousands of people.[181]

---

[179] Unpublished letter from William S. Sadler to Harry P. Harrison, October 4, 1910, Talent file, Redpath Collection.

[180] Martin P. Anderson, Wesley Lewis, and James Murray, *The Speaker and His Audience* (New York: Harper and Row, 1964), p. 1.

[181] 35These are not exaggerated figures. Sadler stated that his lecture, "Catching and Curing a Cold," was given to "about one hundred thousand people each summer at the leading Chautauquas."; *The Cause and Cure of Colds* (Chicago, 1917), p. v. In the preface to *The Truth About Mind Cure* (Chicago, 1928). Sadler wrote, "This little book is the outgrowth of my lecture on 'Faith and Fear,' and its publication commemorates the one thousandth delivery of this lecture." Estimations of total audiences reached by traveling Chautauquas appears in several histories of the movement: Victoria and Robert Ormond Case, *We Called It Culture: The Story of Chautauqua* (New York, 1948), state in their preface that in 1924 alone, 'an estimated 30,000,000 Americans sat in the brown tents pitched nearby some

People sitting on benches outside of tent, 1910s

People who filed into the Chautauqua tents represented eighty percent of the population: workers, producers, substantial business men and women; walking beside them would be the professional men and women: physicians, lawyers, teachers, nurses, artists; and walking beside them would be the farmers, the tradesmen, the students, the children, and the mothers carrying their babies.[182]

12,000 Main Streets and enjoyed the lectures, music, drama, and other cultural items making up the typical Chautauqua week offering." See also: William S. Sadler, *Long Heads and Round Heads* (Chicago, 1918), p. vii; and William S. Sadler, *Americanitis: Blood Pressure and Nerves* (New York, 1925), p. v.

[182] Frank B. Pearson, "A Close - Up of a Chautauqua Crowd," *The Lyceum Magazine*, XXXV, No. 11 (April, 1926), 5.

A former Chautauqua lecturer who maintained that he had lectured in every state of the Union, revealed that the Chautauqua movement represented rural "hick" culture in the eyes of the city sophisticates. Eastern columnists ridiculed those who were part of this "unconventional movement."[183] Yet, the authentic standards were set on the platform; standards that were simple and wholesome and real, however *naive* and *bourgeois* they seemed to the city sophisticate. Louis J. Alber, onetime president of the affiliated Lyceum and Chautauqua Association, contradicted this ridicule with the claim that, "not only is Chautauqua 'the most American thing in America,' but it is the most democratic thing in democracy."[184] Chautauqua was the poor man's university because its particular field served the more remote and smaller communities of the country; it was their only link with culture.[185] It was not until the census of 1920 that America was shown to be an urban society for prior to that time the majority of its citizens were still residents of rural America.[186] Lack of funds and limited access to travel prevented these country people from

LOUIS J. ALBER

---

[183] J. Francis Kee, "History of the Clear Like, Iowa Chautauqua" (unpublished Master's thesis, State University of Iowa, 1939), p. 43.
[184] Mason, "Talk in Chautauqua," p. 419.
[185] Ibid, p. 420.
[186] Thomlinson, *Population*, p. 276.

receiving any other similar opportunity for mental rejuvenation.

The Chautauqua programs strove to teach serious phases of life's endeavor, from "better cooperation in church and school, better teamwork in fighting drink and graft and crime, and better music and literature in the parlor, to better food in the kitchen and better vegetables in prettier gardens."[187]

When an auditor came to the Chautauqua tent and invested two dollars in a ticket, he expected to be amused but he demanded educational "uplift." Keith Vawter said:

> Our merchandise is entertainment and education in such a mixture as will carry the highest percent of education to the least percent of entertainment and pay expenses. A strictly educational program cannot be made a financial success.
>
> ... the lecture is the backbone of our Chautauqua programs. It is what holds our best people and gets our return contracts, but they are not the money producing features of a program. A popular lecturer will draw as high as $11 to $13 per day at the gate. [In addition to his regular salary.][188]

The circuits tried to find speakers with reputations. Many men of national prominence became Chautauqua orators: six presidents of the United States had been listed on the programs, college professors, eminent clergymen, doctors

---

[187] Arthur Pierce Vaughn, "Circuit Riding with the Big Brown Tops," *The Continent*, XLIX, No. 35 (August 29, 1918), 969. Hereafter cited as Vaughn, "Circuit Riding."
[188] Keith Sawter Speech, p. 7.

of philosophy, lawyers, statesmen, scientists, authors, artists and others who were famous in their respective fields spoke to these country audiences. However, all lecturers were tested and approved by the bureau managers before they received contracts.[189]

Along with the attraction provided by famous names, Chautauqua audiences had opportunities to hear important issues of the day expertly presented. There were the political issues debated by such men as Bryan and LaFollette; there were the moral issues usually extolling the methods of clean living and the dangers of demon rum. There were also the international issues, notably America's response in World War I but also informative travelogs presented by world travelers.

Chautauqua promoters were aware that, as important as oratory was, pure lecture programs would have lessened appeal than programs which were liberally balanced with a calculated apportionment of light entertainment. This wisdom led to the inclusion of singers, instrumentalists, humorists, magicians, bell ringers and other entertainers on every program. Dramatic presentations also became a standard feature of the traveling Chautauquas."[190] One manager of the Chautauqua said, "I give a mixture of what people want and what they ought to have. We include as much of the former as we have to have, and as much of the latter as we dare."[191]

The Chautauqua ethic was a moral one; it conformed to

---

[189] Devlin, "Lecturing," p. 1.
[190] "Chautauqua Program," Big Stone Lake, South Dakota, July 3, 1917 to July 9, 1917.
[191] Some Chautauqua Facts, p. 17.

the mores of the communities which it served. The concepts of the small community were based upon Victorian puritanism which was engendered by the church and the home. Their ideation of virtue was sexual purity, hard work and honesty.[192] "Bred in their bones is the Puritan instinct that Fun and Sin are two names for the same Devil."[193] The managers believed that the public must be shielded against the ancient evil of liquor and the evil of cigarettes. Early in the history of the circuits, Keith Vawter expressed his opposition to a lecturer who had become, in his point of view, a "cigarette fiend." Drinking in any company was grounds for dismissal.[194]

Even though the bureaus would boast concerning the freedom of their platforms and state that they had no desire to dictate what any lecturer should say, other than that his speech should pass the test of patriotism and be non - sectarian and non - partisan[195] there was a tacit understanding that this was a "dry" platform and that only "dry" orators would be applauded.[196]

> *So vital is this matter of private morals that the managers of the larger Chautauqua booking bureaus are wont to send form letters to their talent, warning them to avoid as the pestilence anything falling*

---

[192] Donald Linton Graham, "Circuit Chautauqua, Middle Western Institution" (unpublished Doctor's dissertation, State University of Iowa, 1953), p. 182. Hereafter cited as Graham, unpublished dissertation.

[193] Gregory Mason, "Chautauqua: Its Technic," *The American Mercury*, I, No. 3 (March, 1924), 275. Hereafter cited as Mason, "Chautauqua: Its Technic."

[194] Graham, unpublished dissertation, pp. 184 - 185.

[195] E. L. Matthews, "Ideals and Cooperation in the Field," *The Lyceum Magazine*, XXX, No. 1 (December, 1920), 15 - 16.

[196] Frank Bohn.) "America Revealed in Its Chautauqua," Thornton Collection, p. 18.

> within the bucolic definition of immorality. Official sanction for this attitude is given by the Chautauqua Managers' Association, stipulating that a lecturer's contract may be broken at the manager's will if the lecturer conducts himself improperly, i.e., in violation of agricultural mores.[197]

For similar reasons popular music – jazz - was taboo.[198] The circuits gave the rural audiences and small town folks the latest and best things from Broadway; however, these plays were of the clean, wholesome type, "sans bedroom scenes, sordid domestic wrangles and chorus-girl gold diggers."[199] When a play was approved for a Chautauqua audience, it needed no further censorship. MacLaren reported that on one summer circuit in Kansas, alterations in the presentation of *Carmen* portrayed the heroine as working in a dairy instead of a cigarette factory.[200]

In an address to the International Lyceum and Chautauqua Association, Sadler described the importance of Chautauqua morality. In his speech he stated that he wanted to:

> ... impress the young generation of Chautauquans with the seriousness - may I even say, sacredness of their calling. Lack of moral character and ethical standing may not always seriously handicap an actress, entertainer or musician on the American stage today, but such a lack of moral worth is, and I believe always will be, sufficient cause for disbarment from the platform of the American Chautauqua.[201]

---

[197] Mason, "Chautauqua: Its Technic," pp. 276 - 277.
[198] Edna Erie Wilson, "Amusement a La Carte," *The Designer and the Woman's Magazine* (February, 1923), p. 52. Hereafter cited as Wilson, "Amusement a La Carte."
[199] Ibid.
[200] MacLaren, Morally We Roll Along, p. 151.
[201] Mason, "Chautauqua: Its Technic," p. 277.

Thus, the Chautauquas assumed an identity as conservative, moralistic, and religious; as will be pointed out later, this self-portrayal and the tenacity with which it was maintained was to become partially responsible for its own demise.

Paradoxically, it became necessary for the Chautauqua circuits to violate one of the most deeply entrenched of American moral and religious traditions - the observance of the Sunday sabbath. In the interest of the bureau and because of the necessity to facilitate the smooth operation of the schedule, the Chautauqua circuits were organized without regard to the day of the week. Some eastern circuits removed Sunday admission prices thus avoiding the taint of commercialism; however, they asked for voluntary contributions. In the eastern circuits this sometimes brought a greater return; in the midwest, however, the patrons were less willing to contribute and a few circuits found it necessary to cancel Sunday programs.[202] Some circuits merely changed the set of their Sunday program by having the lecturers add a few golden Bible texts to their speeches.[203]

For such occasions, Sadler offered an altered version of his health lecture entitled "Health and Righteousness."[204]
From its beginning until after World War I when its influence began to decline, the Chautauqua platform was a major source of opinion and information for a large number of Americans. That it was a culture forming as well as

---

[202] Graham, unpublished dissertation, pp. 192 - 195.
[203] Mason, "Chautauqua: Its Technic," p. 276.
[204] In Sadler's program brochure, *The Sadlers Popular Health Lectures* (Chicago: W. M. King Printing Service). Hereafter cited as Sadler, *Popular Health Lectures*.

a culture formed institution seems to be indicated by the views of its contemporaries. Community leaders saw it as a promoter of moral uplift and a provider of mental enrichment. In rural sections of America the brown tent was awaited and eagerly welcomed. Farmers planned their work accordingly so that nothing would interfere with Chautauqua week. Women, having too little recreation, forgot about their drudgery as they enjoyed the stimulation of music and laughter. Chautauqua week actually seemed to redeem many towns from dullness and stagnation. One citizen commented: "Chautauqua rendered us a good service this year. We were dead when it came, but we were whooping it up when it left."[205] This institution fulfilled a need of small towns isolated from the world. Reportedly, the contract signers decided to support the Chautauqua because it was an educational and inspirational force in their community. The Seattle Press, in 1917, revealed "many of the patrons declare that they received the value of the season ticket from a single lecture more than once.[206] In some areas, high school students would be given tickets in order that they might be able to take notes and then make reports on the lectures given.[207]

The Chautauqua was also considered to be a national institution and a recognized force for the advancement of national thought and ideals. Many leaders of American life saw it as a significant platform for good. Theodore Roosevelt called Chautauqua "the most distinctly American

---

[205] Wilson, "Amusement a La Carte," p. 52.
[206] H. H. Kennedy, "The Lecturer as a Featured Attraction on the Chautauqua," *Yearbook*, A Record of the Proceedings of the Fifteenth Annual Convention, VII (September 15 - 20, 1917), Miscellaneous Records, Chautauqua Collections. Hereafter cited as Kennedy, *Yearbook*.
[207] *Twenty Years of Progress: 1904-1923*

institution."²⁰⁸ Charles E. Hughes, former Secretary of State, said: "The Chautauqua movement has been one of the most influential of our democratic endeavors."²⁰⁹ President Wilson pronounced his approval saying, "Let me express the hope that the people will not fail in the support of a patriotic institution that may be said to be an integral part of the national defense."²¹⁰ "What I have seen of public life," said Gifford Pinchot of Pennsylvania, "gives me a realizing sense of the power of the Chautauqua movement to mould public opinion."²¹¹ Thomas A. Edison added his words of praise calling the Chautauqua a "movement which has spread over the whole of our country, in fact, over the world; an ideal to be of immense educational value to all the people and of first importance to their welfare."²¹² Chautauqua leaders believed that the lecture platform could be a very effective promoter of patriotism and pro-war sentiment. In the summer of 1917, the wide-spread influence of traveling Chautauquas carried the propaganda of enthusiastic support for the war effort to thousands of communities and to millions of citizens. Louis J. Alber, in an article entitled, "Making Up America's Mind," described the Chautauqua strategy:

> *Every Chautauqua gathering this summer [1917] will be a patriotic rally, and the services of the Chautauqua platform have been placed unreservedly at the call of the Government. There is no more effective way of reaching the people and effecting a solidarity of opinion than is thus offered.*²¹³

---

²⁰⁸ *Some Chautauqua Facts*, p. 1.
²⁰⁹ Ibid.
²¹⁰ "What Notable Men Have Said About Chautauqua," in *Some Chautauqua Facts*.
²¹¹ Ibid.
²¹² *Some Chautauqua Facts*.
²¹³ Louis J. Alber, "Making Up America's Mind," *The Independent*, XC

93

"Every energy," Alber continued, "will be devoted to sounding a high patriotic note."[214] Government officials felt that if the Chautauqua was needed in peace, it was needed more in the time of war because the people of America needed clear thinking and high ideals.[215] Lecturers who had been signed up for various circuits spent a week in Washington to be briefed by returned ambassadors from war capitols, members of the food administration, and by university experts in social and economic matters. While on the circuit, these lecturers continually received up-to-date information.[216] Referring to these patriotic services, Charles Horner of the Redpath-Horner Bureau wrote, in May of 1917: "It is our privilege and our duty to wield a great influence in promoting the patriotic feeling of the country. Not the patriotism that makes people send telegrams ... that awakens desires ... to actually serve the country."[217]

Since lecture was the strength of the Chautauqua, the lecturer had to appeal to the solid, thinking, and forward-looking citizens who signed the guarantees for the ensuing year. As audiences became more and more critical they requested higher grade attractions.

The managers were well aware that it would never pay them to use inferior talent on a Chautauqua program since the audience tended to evaluate the entire program by its weakest feature. In those days the Chautauqua audiences

---

(June 9, 1917), p. 475.
[214] Ibid
[215] "The Lyceum and Chautauqua's Great Opportunity," *The Lyceum Magazine*, XXVI, No. 12 (May, 1917), 10.
[216] Vaughn, "Circuit Riding," p. 969.
[217] Charles F. Homer, "War and Lyceum and Chautauqua: As the Managers View It," *The Lyceum Magazine*, XXVI, No. 12 (May, 1917), 10.

were the origin of public opinion and the program talent often was the basis of these opinions.[218]

The Redpath bureau had evolved a rating system which it called a "grade book." Before the superintendent would leave a town at the end of a Chautauqua program, he would send the names of twenty influential people into the bureau office. The office would immediately mail questionnaires to these individuals and request that they rate the talent. Since these reports were the pulse of the system, they were studied carefully. Only the talent that had high ratings would remain on the program.[219] When it was learned through ratings that a speaker was in demand, Chautauqua bureau managers offered him contracts for return engagements. "It is not so hard to get on the platform as it is to stay there,"[220] managers from the Coit and Alber System pointed out.

The managers used a great deal of time and patience to gradually eliminate the celebrity speakers who were disappointing; they wanted messages that would be of practical value and would serve the vast majority of their audiences. They did not admit anybody to the Chautauqua platform who did not have the training or the experience to deliver a message of genuine, vital and practical interest.[221]

When the Chautauqua idea first took form in upstate New

---

[218] Louis 3. Alber, "Does the Public Want Quality?" *System*, XXXIX (March, 1921), 374.
[219] "Did I Make Good?" *The Lyceum Magazine*, XXXII, No. 2 (April, 1922), 11 - 12.
[220] "The American Magazine Has Chautauqua Story," The *Lyceum* XXXII, No. 2 (July, 1922), 33.
[221] Twenty Years of Progress: 1904-1923.

York, no one could have presaged its phenomenal expansion nor its pervasive influence. And until the visible signs of its decline in the 1920's began to show up in dwindling attendances, unsigned contracts, and diminishing profits, few would have predicted that this American institution was to fall victim to a rapidly changing society and its own fatal identification with a passing age. It would be well to review the apparent causes of its success before elaborating on the causes of its decline and eventual death.

Born in the conservative atmosphere of the Protestant church, the Chautauqua ideal exemplified in its every activity the themes of Mother - Home - and Heaven.[222] It saw itself as a champion of traditional values and a guardian of virtuous sentiments. Chautauquas were welcomed because they guaranteed a combination of serious, sensible oratory and carefully chosen entertainment. For a majority of Americans living away from the large urban centers, intellectual and technological threats to simple life - styles posed no imminent dangers. At the same time, their fascination for the new and the newsworthy, properly interpreted by the selective techniques of Chautauqua managers, brought them day after day and year after year to the tents and assembly halls of Chautauqua centers.

In addition, the Chautauqua platform brought educational benefits to isolated communities at a time when available methods of communication and idea dissemination were still slow and inexact and oratory held an important place in opinion formation, the Chautauqua program offered stimulating and respectable information about the larger world.

---

[222] Bruce Bliven, "Mother, Home and Heaven," *New Republic*, XXXVII (January 9, 1924), 172 - 175.

While Chautauquans avoided identification with worldliness, there was a desire to know more about the changing world. Lectures about science and innovations in areas of health and safety which would bring personal satisfaction and improvement were lauded. To show the beneficial results of increasing knowledge while warding off the threats of scientific materialism demonstrates the particularity with which Chautauqua programs were engineered.

In summary, the Chautauqua success story was written by the cores of leaders and people of talent who followed an ideal and protected it from tarnish. Dedicated to this ideal, they brought vitality to thousands of communities. On the other hand, the success story was also being written by the millions of people who found inspiration and emotional succor, intellectual stimulus and moral reinforcement when they sat in the audiences of Chautauquas everywhere. Frederick William Wile, then chief of the Washington bureau of the Philadelphia Ledger, in 1923, glowingly portrayed the Chautauqua story:

> *I envy the eager attention, the unfeigned interest, the benevolent tolerance Chautauqua extorts from the denizens of the big brown tents. I envy the impression Chautauqua Leaves behind in every community it invades.... If ever I wanted to launch a crusade for the right in this virile nation of ours; if I wanted to reach the heart and soul of America on a great moral issue; if I wanted to stir the emotions of the people at the real fountain - head of national inspiration, I would steer wide of the cities with the teeming, tempestuous millions, and make straight for Main Street" in chautauqua towns.*[223]

---

[223] "Chautauqua Through Journalistic Eyes," *Lyceum Magazine*, XXXIII, No. 9 (February, 1923), pp. 23 - 24.

Chautauqua's decline was unobtrusive and quiet; it simply became less noticed by the press and less needed by the people. Early in the season in 1924, supposedly the "Great Year" of Chautauqua, Keith Vawter wrote to Harry P. Harrison, "If my business was much worse, I would want to join you for Europe with a one way ticket."[224]

The radio brought daily information; the automobile and improved roadways made travel less formidable; the proliferation of local movie houses offered fascinating entertainment with weekly regularity. Along with these innovations came a disintegration of small - town community life.[225] Jazz, the radio, the motion picture and good roads seemed to decree death for the movement, though some attempts were made to recapture the lost glory of earlier days. Where the lecturer had held a dominant place in Chautauqua programs, the spotlight was now turned upon entertainment having a mild degree of sex appeal, a noticeable capitulation to the influence of Hollywood. But the revitalized program brought "new perplexities to the earnest gentlemen who ... invested large sums ..."[226] In 1924 a committee member was reported to have stated, "the people of their town would rather ride in an automobile than attend Chautauqua even if Shakespeare were scheduled to appear in one of his own plays or Paul of Tarsus were on the lecture list."[227] America's taste and life style had changed; Chautauqua, one time considered as a prepotent need, had lost its value.

---

[224] Graham, unpublished dissertation, p. 246.
[225] R. B. Tozier, "A Short Life - History of the Chautauqua," *The American Journal of Sociology*, XL, No. 1 (July, 1934), 72 - 73. Hereafter cited as Tozier, "A Short Life - History."
[226] 80Henry F. Pringle, "Chautauqua In the Jazz Age," *The American Mercury*, XVI (1920), 85 - 86.
[227] Graham, unpublished dissertation, p. 263.

When, in 1932, all circuit Chautauquas were forced to fold their tents,[228] the Chautauqua had left an indelible mark on the life of American society. Some viewed its passing with remorse; accolades were forthcoming. Edwin S. Slossom reminisced:

> *If I were a cartoonist, I should symbolize Chautauqua by a tall Greek goddess, a sylvan goddess, with leaves in her hair - not vine leaves but oak, and tearing open the bars of a cage wherein had been confined a bird, say an owl, labeled "Learning." For that is what Chautauqua has done for the world - it has turned learning loose.*[229]

Not all agreed with this view. After visiting the original setting at Chautauqua Lake, William James criticized the antiseptic character of Chautauqua:

> *This order is too tame, this culture too second-rate; this goodness too uninspiring. This human drama without a villain or a pang; this community so refined that ice-cream soda-water is the utmost offering it can make to the brute animal in man; this city simmering in the tepid lakeside sun; this atrocious harmlessness of all things, - I cannot abide them. Let me take my chances again in the big outside worldly wilderness with all its sins and sufferings. There are heights and depths, the precipices and the steep ideals, the gleams of the awful and the infinite; and there is more hope and help a thousand times than in this dead level and quintessence of every mediocrity.*[230]

In 1932, R. B. Tozier wrote a fitting eulogy:

---

[228] Gay MacLaren, "Morally We Roll Along --to Chautauqua," *Atlantic Monthly*, XVI (May, 1938), 673.
[229] Elizabeth Vincent, "Old First Night," p. 95.
[230] Mason, "Chautauqua: Its Technic," p. 280.

The circuit Chautauqua, having made its last stand in a few widely scattered rural towns, apparently has no offspring; and with its passing there will be no institution remaining as a memento of its former glory.[231]

---

[231] Tozier, "A Short Life - History," p. 73.

IV. THE AUDIENCE

"Chautauqua Audience inside Tent; Corning, Iowa, 1913," *Travelling Culture: Circuit Chautauqua in the Twentieth Century*

The Chautauqua audience was a unique entity in American life; lecturers believed that it was not only the most honest assemblage of Americans but also one of the most exacting. These auditors, which were a true cross section of rural America, had a strong belief in the Sabbath, in the Volstead Act, and in hard work. They respected lecturers who did not violate these norms. Heterogeneous in age, the audience ranged from nine weeks to ninety years. This fact alone tested the versatility of the orator.

Although such audiences hoped to be informed and enlightened, they definitely expected to be entertained. The lecturer who wished to make a serious point found it necessary to embellish his presentation with examples of wit and humor in order to prompt attentiveness and anticipation in the audience.

Only by joining the interests of both the audience and the orator in some sort of mutual interdependent process could the serious message be successful. Thus, the speaker with a vital message was forced to be convincing but essentially on the audiences terms. Sadler's lectures originated in his serious concern for public health; the Chautauqua crowds provided a logical and fertile audience; each found need fulfillment in the other.

His thesis was simplistic in that all of his lectures advocated the return of living according to the rules of nature. For audience appeal and comprehension, he not only delivered *his* lectures in a popular parlance devoid of medical jargon, but employed histrionics to exemplify the action that his auditors should take when a doctor was not available. His lectures could never be considered timeless because he believed in making them timely for the momentary needs of the audience. Each year as his auditors changed he directed his message to that same end. This was his purpose when he exposed them to the health hazards which accompanied the large Chautauqua gatherings. It was also the reason he exhorted his listeners to have yearly health audits for the purpose of discovering early symptoms of disease.

During World War I, he promoted patriotism by informing the citizens concerning the psychology of the war with Germany. After the war when the women adopted *avant-garde* attitudes concerning the hemline, courtship, sex, smoking and drinking, he directed his speeches toward the interpretation of these changes.

As was shown in the previous chapter, the Chautauqua platform reached a multitude of people; each tent would seat approximately two thousand auditors. The Chautauqua audience was a cosmopolitan crowd; it was a cross - section of

American life. However, the Chautauqua audience was an expectant one:

> Somewhere in the audience are the boys who will go to college if they get the right urge from the platform; there are girls there who will turn their attention from cosmetics to culture -- music or art; ... there is the preacher who has been giving out to his people all year and looks forward eagerly to this chance to refresh his own spirit...

> In every audience there is at least one person who is dreaming of the day when he will be on the Chautauqua platform himself. He may be a local clergyman with a "fine address on Lincoln" ... or it may be some girl who has studied music or dramatic art ...[232]

The women were especially strong supporters and tried to be present at each session. They came in white shirt - waists, carrying their knitting, or more frequently carrying a baby. If a baby cried, there was considerably more sympathy for the mother than for the speaker.[233] One appreciative female auditor commented:

> It is a great thing for us, particularly for us younger women with growing children. There are none of us in this town very rich. Most of us have to do all our work. We have little amusement, and almost never get away from home. The Chautauqua brings us an entire change. We plan for weeks before it. There is hardly a

---

[232] Roy L. Smith, "Human Nature on the Chautauqua Circuit," *The Christian Advocate* (September 11, 1924), pp. 1105-1106. Hereafter cited as Smith, "Human Nature."

[233] 2Ida N. Tarbell, "A Little Look at the People." pp. 606 - 607, and *Atlantic Monthly*, CXIX (Nay, 1917), 602 - 610. Hereafter cited as Tarbell, "A Little Look at the People."

> woman I know in town who has not her work so arranged, her pantry so full of food ... [because] she gets her work done up for Chautauqua week.[234]

Thus, the relief from monotony was one reason that the audience gave such enthusiastic support to the Chautauqua. Other auditors felt that it was a tonic for the community; the lecturers gave them something to talk about the rest of the year; still others believed that the platform was an antidote to the traveling carnival that encouraged their boys in evil ways and enticed their girls. Still others looked forward to its prohibition emphasis that "was lessening the power of the saloon."[235]

The audience judged a performer during his first five minutes; there was no mercy. It was crucial that the veteran lecturer, therefore, start immediately to win their good will. The Chautauqua audience would never allow a speaker to rest on laurels already won. Each new audience was a new challenge, and the speaker stood or fell on the basis of the performance of the moment.[236] The audience was eager to learn, but critical. One lecturer commented after many performances:

> One gets an impression of being "sized up," quite commonly and quite naturally. They are people who have something to do, responsibilities that they regard as grave, work that they know is necessary.... They think about what you say, but you may or may not influence the opinions which they hold.[237]

The auditors were honest and forthright; never would they sit through a lecture to be polite. If they did not agree with the speaker's opinions, or if they thought he was boring, they simply stood up and walked out of the tent.

---

[234] Ibid.
[235] Ibid, p. 608.
[236] 5Smith, "Human Nature," p. 1105.
[237] Ibid

One veteran lecturer recalled his moments on the platform:

> *Some audiences bear you onward buoyantly, begging you to do your best, and some are Sargasso Seas and you plow through them "while they sit and look at you curiously, without listening ...*[238]

Sadler's audience had the qualifications for his mission. Their medical knowledge was unsophisticated as there was little literature available for the laity -- no health articles in the newspapers; they had little access to information on preventive medicine, first - aid, etc. The following are some of the questions that people asked concerning their health:

> *What can I eat to reduce? How many times a week should meat be included in the diet? ... Is uncooked food better than cooked food? ... Should coffee be eliminated in case of a weak heart? ... Is it necessary to eat three times a day? ... What foods are best for perfect assimilation and for perfect elimination of waste from the body?*[239]

Other questions concerned the amount of iodine that should be taken for goiter, the causes of pimples, the causes of nervousness, the feasibility of wearing corsets and high heels, and the necessity of tonsil removal. However, with the growth of patent medicine, advertisements of pills and elixirs in the newspapers had become a public menace. The newspapers daily heralded the cures of patent medicine; many newspapers were sustained by such drug advertisements.[240] At best Sadler's audiences had not been subjected to correct information. Too

---

[238] Ellerbe and Ellerbe, "The Most American Thing," p. 444.
[239] Lydia Allen Devilbiss, "What People Want to Know About Their Health," Part I, *Hygeia*, II (July, 1924), 435. Hereafter cited as Devilbiss, "What People Want to Know."
[240] Pickard and Buley, *Midwest Pioneers*, p. 268.

many pills were being offered after illness occurred, and there was no emphasis on preventive medicine or the concern about staying well. Sadler felt that the practice of medicine has long been shackled with superstition and handicapped with the ignorance and uncertainties of empiricism. The ... century will probably go down in history as an era of promiscuous drugging"[241]

Sadler urged the people to practice preventive medicine; he awakened them to become aware of their bodies and to practice effective health habits. He urged that prevention was better than cure; he suggested that the "health audit" or yearly physical check - up was analogous to taking care of their car.

> No automobilist would dare to drive his machine forward heedlessly and carelessly with no thought of periodic inspection and without proper oiling and care at regular intervals, unless his journey were one actually of life and death; and yet how often do we observe intelligent men and women urging their body - machines forward heedlessly and carelessly under the lash of greed and ambition, utterly disregarding disease possibilities and utterly blind to the danger signals of disease which are to loom up so soon in the pathway of life just ahead.

> The higher the speed, the more intensely you drive the human machine, the more the necessity that the bodily mechanism should be regularly inspected. Many a man thinks nothing of spending from twenty - five to one hundred dollars, periodically, for having his automobile overhauled and kept in first - class running order. At the same time, he is not willing to invest even half that amount in the all - important business of periodically inspecting and annually overhauling his own physical body -- his nervous, digestive, circulatory and eliminative mechanisms.[242]

---

[241] Sadler, *Mind Cure*, p. 27.
[242] William S. Sadler, "The Practice of Preventive Medicine," *Illinois Medical Journal*, XXXIV, No. 3 (September, 1918), 114 - 115.Speech presented at

His speech concerning "The Practice of Preventive Medicine," must have had impact as he spoke about self - preservation:

> *We have but one set of vital machinery to run us a lifetime, and when, through neglect, it "goes stale," we have to make out with what we have left.*[243]

Sadler advocated the reform of living habits and found his audience eager for this information that promised better health and longer life. He challenged them:

> *What do the intelligent men and women today, who are neglecting to find out about the workings and behavior of their vital mechanisms, think of the engineer who never inspected his machinery until he got word of a breakdown? What do you think of the business man who never audited his books until informed that his cashier had left for Canada? What is the situation of a nation that never prepares for war until hostilities break out; and what estimate can we put upon the intelligence and forethought of men and women who never have their body - machines inspected until a physical breakdown or a nervous blow - up hurries them into the hands of a doctor or off to a sanitarium?*[244]

Sadler was not only a pioneer as a medic orator, but he also had the zeal of a reformer. His interests were in sympathy with Ralph Waldo Emerson's image of a reformer:

> *What is a man born for, but to be a Reformer, a Remaker of what man has made ... imitating that great Nature which embosoms us all, and which sleeps no moment on an old past, but every hour repairs herself, yielding*

---

the sixty - eighth annual meeting of- the Illinois State Medical Society at Springfield, May 22, 1918.
[243] Ibid.
[244] Sadler, "The Practice of Preventive Medicine," P. 115.

us every morning a new day, and with every pulsating a new life?[245]

By 1907, the *Lyceumite and Talent magazine* displayed a complete page of promotional literature sponsored by the Mutual Lyceum Bureau which listed the program offerings of Sadler.

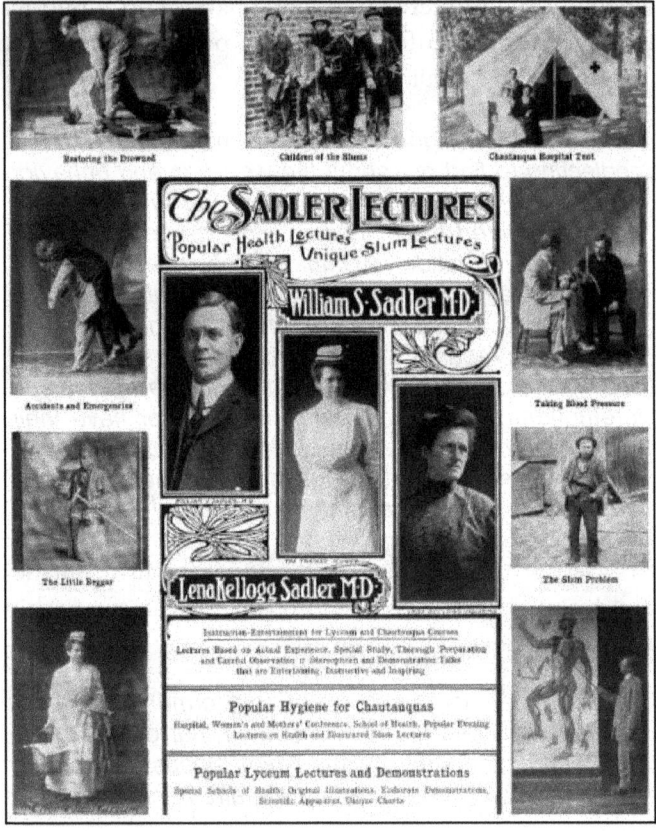

It promised to interested Chautauqua and Lyceum audiences:

---

[245] Ralph Waldo Emerson, "Man the Reformer," *Natures Addresses,* and Lectures, I of *The Complete Works of Ralph Waldo Emerson* (Boston: Houghton, Mifflin, 1884), p. 236.

"Lectures Based on Actual Experience, Special Study, Thorough Preparation and Careful Observation: Stereopticon and Demonstration Talks that are Entertaining, Instructive and Inspiring."[246] With this announcement Sadler's Chautauqua career was publicly launched. Although he had delivered occasional lectures prior to his graduation but because of his caution concerning medical ethics had avoided attracting publicity, now he began to solicit speaking engagements on a broader scale. Evidence of this exists in the form of a letter to Harry P. Harrison, manager of the Redpath Lyceum Bureau:

> *I am writing at this time to ask if it would be possible for you to arrange for me to give two or more lectures at a time and place to suit your convenience between now and Christmas that you might hear my work... I am sending you a couple of my books that you might see something of my status and standing...* [247]

Harrison replied to Sadler on October 11, 1910:

> *Mr. Crotty, assistant manager, tells me that there are one or two churches here that he could arrange a date in at practically any time. They are unable to pay anything, simply furnish the audience. If this is what you mean, simply let us know and we will put him on the job so that we will got [sic] an opportunity to hear your work.*[17]

It is significant to note in this letter the specific mention that such services were to be rendered gratis.

The only factual information that could be found concerning

---

[246] "The Sadler Lectures: Popular Health Lectures, Unique Slum Lectures," *Lyceumite* & *Talent*, V and VI (September 1907), 2, inside cover.

[247] Unpublished letter from William S. Sadler to Harry P. Harrison, October 4, 1910, Talent file, Redpath Collection.

Sadler's fee or stipends received on the Chautauqua circuit were listed in an unpublished Master's thesis, "The Chautauqua in Des Moines County, Iowa." According to Helen Gladstone Nau's research, Sadler and his wife, Dr. Lena, received $170 in salary for their two lectures and the afternoon round table on this specific circuit in 1922 in Des Moines County. In comparison, uneducated, unordained Billy Sunday with his non - authoritative "acrobatic preaching"[248] asked for and received $375 for an individual lecture in 1930.[249] William Jennings Bryan was making $227.10 per lecture in 1921 on this same circuit.[250]

As other lecturers had discovered, the Chautauqua audience proved to be a very special audience. Speakers soon learned that "honest - to-God Americans live in small towns."[251] "The salt of the earth it is -- good, kindly, wholesome American"[252] was another label attached to this unique audience. In the words of Charles F. Homer, the "basic idea of the Chautauqua was to give the speaker his hour."

> *No whistling nor clapping of hands nor signs at the reluctant but final bows of the entertainers and male quartette could serve to delay the Lecturer, or to lessen his importance. He was the force that made sponsors labor without stint, neglect their own affairs and face peril of paying deficits.*[253]

---

[248] Robert T. Oliver, *History of Public Speaking in America* (Boston: Allyn and Bacon, Inc., 1966), p. 391.

[249] Helen Gladstone Nau, "The Chautauqua in Des Moines County, Iowa" (unpublished Master's thesis, State University of Iowa, 1937), p. 196.

[250] Ibid. p. 199.

[251] Frederick William Wile, "Chautauqua Through Journalistic Eyes," *The Lyceum Magazine*, XXXIII, No. 9 (February, 1923), 24.

[252] Elizabeth Vincent, "Old First Night," p. 96.

[253] Charles F. Homer, "Chautauqua People Are Pretty Good," unpublished notes, Chautauqua Collection, University of Iowa, p.9.

If a lecturer was effective in the eyes of his audience, he could hold them for one and a half hours in a one hundred five degree tent. However, heat was less of a distraction than other inside and outside stimuli. The tent was open on all sides; children sat down in the front seats; they circulated freely throughout the audience whispering loudly to each other. Sometimes they took liberties with the speaker, e.g., reaching over the foot lights and untieing [sic] his shoes.[254] An adventurous young boy sometimes climbed the tent pole during a lecture and a crew boy would have to bring him down. Occasionally, an aged auditor would go to sleep and fall off of his chair.[255] It was not an unusual occurrence for a dog or a cat to wander across the platform.

The audience only saw the lecturer; they looked into his face to study his eyes, to watch his action to determine whether his life entitled him to their confidence. These rural residents had a sincere appreciation for speakers who had had struggles in their own lives, and who understood that the farmer's life style was a rigorous one in the early 1900's. In one advertising circular promoting the lectures of Sadler the thought that here was a man that who knew work as they did was emphasized:

> Dr. Sadler is a good example of his own teachings -- he is a hard worker, but a simple liver. His diversified labors as surgeon, author, teacher, and lecturer, not to mention his sociological and psychological investigations, keep him exceedingly busy for about fifteen hours a day.[256]

When managers were announcing the coming of a new performer or lecturer they began building his reputation and moral

---

[254] Gregory Mason, "Talk in Chautauqua," p. 418.
[255] Ellerbe and Ellerbe, "The Most American Thing."
[256] "Personal: Dr. William S. Sadler, Surgeon, Author, and Teacher," *The Lyceumite and Talent*, V, No. 3 (August, 1911), 7.

character to coincide with the norms of the audience. For example, they related that Sadler was a Christian by stating:

> We've been told that when he is garbed in white and the helpers stand ready while the anesthetic is being administered, before he uses the knife all pause for a moment and with bowed heads a prayer is sent up that the higher Wisdom and the infallible Hand may direct the blade.[257]

The auditors were likewise informed that Sadler was a "dry" orator: "Dr. Sadler stands by his principles, even to the turning down of his wine - glass at some medical banquet."[258] His affinity for the "dry" flavor of Chautauqua was established.

When superintendents of the individual Chautauquas introduced a new speaker they tended to use hyperbolic emotional appeal in order to create the proper sat for the speaker. For ethical reasons Sadler would always ask that the local physician introduce him. On one occasion Sadler was introduced in this manner to demonstrate his acquaintanceship with hard work -- a commendable ethic.

> A man is immortal until his work is done. The proof of it? Take the case of this boy, underweight and slighted by nature.
>
> Fortune and Destiny saw the slight and tried to make it up by giving the boy an extra lot of mental capacity. How often it happens -- a great soul in an insignificant body, a tremendous steam capacity in an engine that can't carry it. Hence, so many vital explosions.

---

[257] "Message For the Masses," p. 33.
[258] Ibid

> *It was a struggle with little health and less money to get an education. He plunged headlong into his work, sometimes forgetting to eat or sleep. He became a discoverer -- and a wreck. He was told to quit, to change his work, to go out west and save the shreds of his constitution. But he kept at work and tho now only in his thirties has lived a lifetime since then. It simply made him balance up his life and learn how to repair the machine while running. It has been the world's gain, for William S. Sadler has become a beacon - light to the thousands of victims of the high- pressure life. In this age of "Amencanitis" he has become the great teacher of the balanced life - how to repair the machine while carrying the over load. He has become an author who speaks with authority, for he is head of his department in a well-known Medical School of Chicago. Here come hundreds of physicians each year to be shown by this young teacher the modern treatment of disease without drugs - and this, mind you, achieved in the regular channels of his profession.... He is preaching to the physician as to the masses how to prevent disease and to cure it by natural methods.*[259]

One of the basic themes in all of Sadler's speaking was the return to living according to the rules of nature. When he began speaking in 1905 he coined the term "Americanitis" and used it as his speech title; "Americanitis" was equated with high pressure living which was characteristic of the American citizen. He subsequently delivered this speech "more than five hundred times to Chautauqua audiences throughout the United States."[260] He instructed his audiences to learn how to control and how to live with a nervous temperament. "Remember that the 'leopard cannot change his spots, nor the Ethiopian his skin,' but these nervous folks can learn to live so

---

[259] "Message for the Masses," p. 33.
[260] Sadler, *Americanitis*, pp. v - vi.

as to prevent blow - ups and breakdowns."[261] It was his contention that nature alone could cure many diseases, if given the time, without the aid of a doctor. He was eager to denounce patent medicine from the Chautauqua platform; he waged his own professional war on the "pill factories" and the makers of the elixirs with the red label.[262]

Over 5,000 questions were submitted by audiences in forums following health lectures; these questions indicated that the greatest health problem of the American family was to know how and what to eat. More than one - third of the questions asked related to diet. Another one - third revealed a concern about disease, i.e., communicable, kidney, high blood pressure, and other organic problems. A large number of the questions were classified as symptomatic, e.g., they asked the causes of shortness of breath, the cure for nervousness, the effect of over-fatigue, the causes of headache, etc.[263]

Sadler touched upon all of these questions in his basic laws of health. It is the belief of the writer that he outlined these laws to almost every Chautauqua audience because they appear again and again in his lectures that were developed into book form. Sadler's laws of health were his prerequisites for all preventive medicine.

He stated that the outdoor life with its fresh air and sunshine was vital to the human being:

> Man is an outdoor animal. He was made to live in a garden -- not a house.... Consumption (tuberculosis), pneumonia, bronchitis and catarrh are house diseases

---

[261] Sadler, *Americanitis*, p. 71.
[262] "Message For the Masses," p. 33.
[263] Devilbiss, "What People Want to Know," pp. 435 - 436

> *... sunshine is the only known substance that will effectually kill disease germs and yet in no way harm the human body.*
>
> *Oxygen is the vital fire of life.... Without oxygen, digested food is just as useless as is the coal in the furnace when all the drafts are closed down.... Sleep out of doors is a preventive, as well as a cure, for tuberculosis.*[264]

In 1909 Sadler displayed an ecological concern about a growing problem of air pollution; he suggested a reform because he believed "foul air was the curse of modern manufacturing."[265]

He believed that the people should begin a crusade against impure air as physicians attributed impure air as the underlying cause or at least the beginning of consumption or pneumonia. The importance of fresh air was made explicit with statistics which revealed that one death out of every four or five represented a death from consumption or pneumonia. Sadler exhorted the platformist and the audience to become familiar with the basic principles underlying the science of ventilation.[266]

> *Many a lecturer has been reported a partial failure because he could not arouse enthusiasm and entertain his audience, for the simple reason that they were anesthetized - semi-chloroformed - from the repeated breathing of the foul and poisoned atmosphere of the lecture hall. Again, no lecturer or entertainer can do his best work*

---

[264] William S. Sadler, "For a Long Life in the Lyceum: The Platformist's Physical Efficiency in a Nutshell -- A Bird's Eye View of the Laws of Health," Part I, *The Lyceumite*, VII and *Talent*, XIX, No. 27 (August, 1909), p. 10. Hereafter cited as Sadler, "For a Long Life," Part I.

[265] William S. Sadler, "Give Your Audience Fresh Air," *The Lyceumite and Talent*, III, No. 8 (January, 1910), pp. 9 - 10.

[266] Ibid.

> when his own system is surcharged - literally saturated with the poison produced not only by his own body, but also by the respiratory exhalations of the audience. [267]

He argued for the use of better ventilation in the city schools as he felt this was actually stunting children's growth patterns. In many lectures he admonished the atrocious ventilation of churches:

> During the last century, it was recorded that the air became so foul in the churches during midwinter revivals that at a late hour the candles would go out, because of the exhaustion of oxygen - the mourners and worshippers regarding this as an evidence of God's displeasure with sinners... [268]

Sadler's third law of nature dealt with the use of muscular exercise:

> Man is a working machine. The study of anatomy seems to indicate that he was never made to sit down ... The ideal exercise is walking five to ten miles a day out of doors, with the arms swinging freely ... Systematic physical exercise is absolutely essential to good circulation and sound digestion. [269]

The scientific and sensible wearing of clothing was the basis of Sadler's fourth law:

> Clothing should be physiological and anatomic; that is, the clothes should be made to fit the body, and not the body to fit the clothes.... Constrictions of the waist, as by the modern corset, favor liver and gall - stone disorders, together with stomach trouble, constipation, and other

---

[267] Sadler, "Give Your Audience Fresh Air," pp. 9 - 10.
[268] William S. Sadler, *The Science of Living* (Chicago: Thomas S. Rockwell Company, 1930), p. 277.
[269] Sadler, "For A Long Life," Part I, p. 11.

serious diseases... Corsets worn by women, and tight belts by men interfere with natural and normal respiration and weaken the abdominal muscles.[270]

The mechanics of eating was his fifth law:

Engineers know how to feed their furnaces better, and farmers know how to feed their cattle better, than the average man knows how to feed his own body.

A lot of foods are better eaten raw... the original diet of primitive man consisted largely of the things that grow out of the earth and upon trees.

Apply the eight - hour rule to the stomach and it will seldom strike; that is, allow eight hours between regular meals, and put nothing into the stomach between meals.[271]

In his lectures he cautioned his auditors concerning the use of highly seasoned dishes and strong condiments as he believed that vinegar was as dangerous as alcohol for damaging the liver. He had a favorite epigram, "Look with disfavor on anything that is hot when it is cold."[272]

His sixth law concerning the drinking of pure water or "Adam's Ale" was repeated at each health lecture. He believed that it was essential to cleanse oneself on the inside as well as on the outside. Concerning the mouth and the teeth, he created a humorous epigram: "At the rate dentists are putting gold into human teeth, the future gold mines will be in the graveyards."[273]

---

[270] Sadler, "For A Long Life," Part I, p. 11.
[271] William S. Sadler, "For A Long Life in the Lyceum," Part II, *The Lyceumite*, VII and *Talent*, XIX, No. 20 (October, 1909), 8.
[272] Theme used in all of Sadler's health lectures and books.
[273] Sadler, "For A Long Life in the Lyceum," Part II, p. 9.

In his last two laws of nature, Sadler promoted the essentials of regular bathing and adequate sleep. He said that regular bathing was "not a luxury, but a necessity"[274] because of the type of clothing people wore and because of the indoor living patterns they followed. One frequently offered suggestion extolled the therapeutic benefits of occasional cold baths. Sleep was called the "antidote for work."[275] Listeners were reminded by Sadler that eight hours of sleep per day would contribute positively to preservation of health. With these simple and easily recalled words of advice he presented helpful health guides for his auditors. The impact of their exposure to such medical advice cannot be measured; however, as in the case of the "Chautauqua Salute," the influence of Sadler's oratory must have been significant.

Sadler postulated that it was his experience with and observation of so many "nervous patients who had been neglected, operated upon, and otherwise mistreated, without being in the least helped,"[276] that led to his further study of psychotherapy. Not only was he interested in the instilling of scientific health habits in the minds of mankind, in the education of the ignorant concerning the structure of the human body, in making people aware of personal hygiene and the dangers of overindulgence, but also in the improving of mental health which he believed was the basic cause of physical illness. Sadler delivered his lecture on "Faith and Fear" to "audiences from Maine to California and from the Canadian Border to the Gulf."[277] It was a popular lecture on mental medicine, his thesis being:

> *It is a physiological fact - a psychological truth - that every time we think a thought the body acts or reacts in*

---

[274] Sadler, "For a Long Life in the Lyceum," Part II, p. 9.
[275] Ibid.
[276] William S. Sadler, *Worry and Nervousness or the Science of Self-Mastery*, p. vii.
[277] Sadler, *Mind Cure*, preface.

> *response to our thinking ... all the functions of the body are more or less disturbed and upset by fear – thought ... Fear, then, becomes the cause of many functional diseases.*
>
> *Mind cure is the real explanation of many an apparent miracle; an understanding of psychotherapy helps us to explain many otherwise mysterious and remarkable cures of human disease.*[278]

One of his favorite epigrams in this lecture was "the world is dying for need of just what you are wasting on yourself; that is, pity, sympathy, and energy."[279]

The challenge of holding a Chautauqua audience took artistry; the audience was relatively polite; however, if the speaker was uninteresting, they openly conveyed negative forms of feedback. It was felt in those times that "to hold an audience spellbound is a thing worth living for."[280] In a visual analysis of the audience one was aware of the heterogeneity under the brown tent. Down in front by the speaker's platform sat rows of children, "among whom ... [were] mingled the few surviving members of the G.A.R."[281] Towards the center sat the fathers and mothers; the last rows were filled with the young couples who were eager for entertainment. Just outside the tent some benches were appropriated for the smokers in the audience; this spot was known as "fumigator's row."[282] One prominent manager expounded, "If you can hold the interest of the last three rows you are a success on the Chautauqua."[283] In order

---

[278] Ibid, pp. 7 - 14.
[279] Ibid, p. 190.
[280] Bart Kennedy, "Audiences the World Over," *The Lyceum Magazine*, XXVI, No. 2 (July, 1916), 21.
[281] Smith, "Human Nature," p. 1105.
[282] Smith, "Human Nature," p. 1105.
[283] Ibid.

for a speaker to remain on the circuit for long, it was necessary for him to have a popular as well as a salient lecture to hold the attention of such a diversified group. Sadler coupled histrionics with his lecture to gain this end.

> Dr. Sadler first gave his lecture on "Americanitis" or the high pressure life. He told us how to work hard and live easy, how to maintain the highest mental efficiency with the least danger of physical explosion. While he talked a trained nurse was giving experiments with a little machine that tested blood pressure on volunteers from the audience. He pictured the effects of nervous strain and mental worry. It was one of those heart - to - heart talks so illuminating as to inspire you with a new desire to work both for your health and for your success in life as never before. It was done in plain English, and with a sincerity that made you want to follow him after wards and ask for more of the same thing.
>
> The last part of the program was a demonstration of how to meet the common emergencies of a household. It was presented in a most realistic manner. There was a scream of pain from down in the audience, and a girl - that inimitable fourth member - was carried upon the stage with her arm apparently shockingly scalded. The Sadlers took her in charge and showed how 'to treat burns in the most approved way'. Hardly was she bandaged when there was an outcry from another part, and a -boy fished out-of the lake was brot [sic] up, apparently drowned. Dr. Sadler began the resuscitation of the lad, all the while emphasizing the necessity of working over these supposed drowned ones for hours before giving up. He stated his belief that scores of lives are lost every season because the rescuers pronounce the body dead, when by prolonged and suitable efforts life might be restored. Then they brot [sic] up a- girl who had fainted.[284]
> "I had no more than gotten her in good condition until some one really did faint. I went to her in a hurry and

---

[284] "Message for the Masses," pp. 32 - 33.

> *promptly brought her around. This was a very fine demonstration of the power of suggestion. Next, someone was supposed to have swallowed poison. A stomach tube was called into play, and the stomach was washed out."*[285] *And so with broken bones and cut arteries, the audience saw what to do while waiting for the doctor.*[286]

According to Sadler's daughter, the display of histrionics with which he concluded his Americanitis lecture proved to be very effective and spectacular. This was a demonstration of the method of transporting a person who had become incapacitated:

> *Dr. Sadler would call for a gentleman to come up to the platform. Well, on one occasion, the gentleman responding weighed around 200 pounds. The doctor, who weighed about 130 pounds at the time, never batted an eye, but told the gentleman to lie down on his back and relax. The doctor then took off his own coat, took a deep breath, and most dexterously landed the 200 pounder on his back and carried him off the platform. Too bad you couldn't have heard the applause of those 5,000 people.*[287]

Audiences in those times took a great interest in the lectures, and it was difficult to discover whether the audiences selected the kind of programs that were to be offered or whether the programs determined the character of their audience.[288]

However, it was clearly evident that the audiences were demanding:

---

[285] Sadler's Papers.
[286] "Message for the Masses," p. 33.
[287] Christy Interview.
[288] Anne Suhm Etty, "What's Wrong With Chautauqua," *The Drama*, XIV (March - April, 1924), 213.

> It was now past the supper hour. The Sadlers were trying to quit, but that audience that had sat on those hard boards for hours cried, "Go on!" Chautauqua audiences are brutal. In a ten - days feast they become mentally bilious and spiritually dyspeptic from the over - feeding. I have heard the great speakers of the nation struggle in vain to hold and feed a crowd already gorged, but I have never seen a chautauqua held up to near the time of the evening hour, as the Sadlers held this one.[59]

Many auditors interviewed the lecturer after the oration was over in order to ask questions. These were blunt, earthy people; if they didn't like the address they generally said so frankly, stated their objections and pointed out what they considered weaknesses.[60] It was generally difficult for Sadler to leave the tent as people wanted to know more about these crucial issues which concerned their foremost motive appeal - self-preservation.

> Long after they [Sadler's group] closed, people lingered about the stage to ply them with questions. Many sufferers came for advice. But here again we run into the doctor and the ethics of his profession. He is not a traveling doctor; he is only out to carry the Gospel of Health to the masses. He refuses absolutely to take pay for advice, and will not consult with a patient while on a lecture tour save on the request of and in the presence of the patient's physician. Their strict adherence to these methods which they call the ethics of the profession has caused the local physicians to become their best friends.[61]

It is apparent that the main goal of this medic orator was to bring to as many people as possible a message which contained helpful advice for health care and prevention of mental and physical breakdown. Although he used the Chautauqua platform extensively for this purpose, his zeal was more than once directed toward the structure of the Chautauqua itself. Sadler insisted that the Chautauqua should be more than a channel of positive information, that it should be an exemplary institution functioning to elevate standards of personal and social hygiene. In keeping with this goal he often exposed the health hazards which accompanied the large gatherings promoted by the Chautauqua program.

Warning of serious disease, he denounced the public drinking cup so common to Chautauqua gatherings. Chautauquans were urged to provide their own collapsible drinking cups and Sadler further provided criteria for determining the potability of the available water. He warned that

> ...pure water containing carbon - dioxide, which comes from the mountain regions, sparkles and bubbles, but all ordinary well water which is found to sparkle, should be condemned at once, as this sparkling is evidence of grave contamination. The water from shallow wells near graveyards nearly always sparkles in this manner.[62]

Sadler challenged platform managers and others responsible for the conditions surrounding the Chautauqua activities to pay more attention to hygienic details and the well being of the patrons rather than to trivia:

> We resent the platform manager's giving all his time to lost jewelry, side combs, handkerchiefs and fans, - telling the people just where they may be found... It is wonderful what machinery the modern chautauqua develops for caring for lost trinkets. Has not the time come for us to develop machinery for caring for lost health, or rather to prevent the loss of health or the contraction of colds, bronchitis, pneumonia, etc.[289]

Noting that audiences sitting day after day in the Chautauqua

---

[289] Sadler, "For Health at the Chautauquas," p. 11.

tent were sometimes exposed to unnecessary dust, Sadler proposed that the floors be sprinkled before being swept to avert the possibility of lung infection and discomfort. He noted also thoughtless placement of the speaker's stand would often force the audience to face the glare of the sun, causing eye strain and fatigue to "the eyes of hundreds, and even thousands."[290] His remedy for this problem was a simple rearrangement of the speaker's platform.

Sadler also attacked the inherent dangers of the eating facilities at these gatherings and fervently appealed that the Chautauqua management give their attention to the securing of a pure milk supply;

> *Every summer thousands of babies are sacrificed to bad milk. Have your milk bought from cows that are inspected; have it supervised, raise the standard, and start the movement for saving the babies...* [291]

He impelled them earnestly to regard with disdain the common house fly; the kitchen and dining pavilion on the Chautauqua grounds should be carefully screened:

> *Young children and others attending the chautauqua and eating food which has been tramped over by these disease-carrying flies, will return home and be forthwith seized with cholera morbus or other bowel disturbances. As many as a million germs are found on one foot of a single fly.* [292]

One of the most hygienic impacts of the medic orator was his ability to quell and finally stop the "Chautauqua salute." Many lecturers were stunned when they had completed their first

---

[290] Ibid.
[291] Ibid, p. 12.
[292] Ibid, p. 10.

Sunday lecture and instead of hearing a thunderous applause, received only visual recognition from the audience; sometimes thousands of handkerchiefs would be waving in the "Chautauqua salute." Harry P. Harrison said that the practice of waving handkerchiefs on Sundays persisted until just before World War I when Sadler put a stop to it.[293]

Sadler's lecture, "Catching and Curing a Cold," "was given to about one hundred thousand people each summer at the leading Chautauquas."[294] He warned his audiences that colds were not only responsible for an enormous pecuniary loss but they lowered the resistance of the individual to more serious diseases:

> Handkerchiefs which have been used by persons suffering from colds and influenza are especially dangerous and should not be carelessly thrown about the house. The practice of using an ordinary handkerchief for giving the "Chautauqua salute" should be discarded.[295]

It is obvious that Sadler believed that the Chautauqua, which, touched the lives of so many, could and should become a model through its practice of hygiene and sanitation.

Return engagements and renewed contracts were concrete evidence that Sadler's lectures were effective in his day. Alfred L. Flude, Manager of the Coit-Alber Chautauqua circuit, highly endorsed Sadler:

> Dr. William S. Sadler was a pioneer in the work of taking the people into the confidence of the medical profession.

---

[293] Harrison, *Culture*, p. 47.
[294] William S. Sadler, *The Cause and Cure of Colds* (Chicago: A.C. McClurg & Co., 1917), pp. vii - viii. Hereafter cited as Sadler, *Cause and Cure*.
[295] Ibid, pp. 49 - 50.

> *His medical mission to the people at once met with a splendid response from Chautauqua audiences everywhere.*
>
> *Very few Chautauqua attractions have ever achieved such an enviable reputation for "making good" and securing such a large percentage of return dates.*
> *In my judgment there is no attraction upon the platform of greater value, and it would be hard to find another attraction which leaves behind so much of practical knowledge and common sense as do the Sadlers.*[296]

Sadler's manager, Wilfred C. Kellogg, in a letter to Harry P. Harrison, wrote:

> *Last year, before signing a contract for the Sadlers to go over [sic] Mr. Holladay's Circuit, I wrote to the leading Chautauqua managers to ascertain how many were interested in securing the Sadlers and such a general interest was expressed that I feel it best this year to communicate with those who expressed such an interest before definite arrangements are finally concluded for the summer of 1918.*[297]

S. M. Holladay, manager of a circuit Chautauqua, gave Sadler an unqualified recommendation. He said Sadler was one of the best lecturers ever appearing in the middle west. He lectured in seventy - seven towns in one summer and his work was high grade, constructive and very profitable to each community.[298]

In 1912 the Chautauqua Manager's Association wrote: "During the past three years this company [Sadler's] has filled twice

---

[296] Flude's Endorsement of the Sadlers," *The Lyceum Magazine*, XXVI (November, 1917), 4.
[297] Unpublished letter from Wilfred C. Kellogg to Harry P. Harrison, September 21, 1917, Redpath Collection, Talent file.
[298] Sadler Brochure, "Popular Health Lectures."

as many return engagements as new ones -- an eloquent proof of both the intrinsic value and the entertaining quality of the attraction."[299]

Sadler's writing career paralleled his lecturing activities, in fact was often inspired by audience response. However, Chautauqua managers never permitted their talent to sell products on the platform. In order to accommodate this policy and the insistent demand from audiences to have his lectures in print, Sadler made arrangements with the Chautauqua Manager's Association to direct the sale of his health books. Not only did he relinquish the profits from his books but also the royalties. He made further arrangements whereby the full profits on the sales of his books were to be turned over to the treasurers of each local Chautauqua.[300]

Except for brief intervals such as the occasion of his study in Europe, Sadler appeared annually on Chautauqua platforms. Sometimes he was under circuit management and other times he acted as an independent agent.

As he developed a growing interest in psychotherapy, his theme of preventive medicine was expanded to include what he termed "preventive mental medicine." With just as much dedication as before he continued his public lecturing.
In his lecturing travels Sadler suffered many of the hardships and discomforts typically faced by Chautauqua talent. On one occasion, e.g., a severe thunderstorm came up during one of his lectures. He recalled this experience with his audience:

> *The program was about over, when one of those thunder and lightning storms with wind and much water*

---

[299] "The Sadler's: A Whole Chautauqua in Themselves," *Lyceum and Talent*, VI, No. 3 (August, 1912), *51*.
[300] Message For the Masses," p. 33.

> struck the big tent and flowed on the ground under it. Lightning struck one of the big poles just in front of the platform. Two women fell over unconscious, several were burned on the legs. I ordered them lifted up on the stage, and they were resuscitated, and burns dressed. No deaths![301]

He remembered other situations. One night when they were driving in Iowa, the car wheels got clogged with the soft mud of the wet roads. Sadler and his small son had to continually get out of the car and dig the mud out of the wheels with their hands in order to keep the car moving.[302]

On another occasion, because their train was delayed, Sadler and his associates were forced to hire a hand car and hand pump their way down the tracks to the next town where their audience was awaiting their message.[303]

While journeying to Chautauqua appointments in the West, Sadler and his family encountered other problems. Sadler reminisced with some relief concerning a dangerous episode which occurred while driving in the mountains of Colorado. At one point his car went off the road and he thought that his entire family would be killed. He recalled that there was not another spot for miles that would have prevented their car from rolling down the cliff. But they were safe and he was able to arrive at his destination in time to speak.[304]

The audiences were not always aware of the difficulties that the talent encountered while traveling to their town; yet, it is reported that the auditors frequently waited far past the scheduled time.

---

[301] Sadler's Papers.
[302] Christy Interview.
[303] Ibid.
[304] Sprunger Interview.

While driving to Eureka, California, for another engagement, Sadler's Ford lost a rear wheel which went unnoticed until they observed it rolling down the road ahead of them. These specific problems were over and above the normal hardships sustained in meeting the schedules and maintaining the neat appearance required by Chautauqua life.[305]

As America prepared for and then entered into World War I, the Chautauqua platform became a part of the propaganda effort to generate loyalty and sacrificial support. Sadler was interested in the promotion of intelligent patriotism; he was desirous that American citizens understood the psychology of the war. In 1918 he wrote to Harry P. Harrison, stating:

> *Several months ago, I became seriously impressed with the fact that a large number of American citizens didn't seem fully to realize what we were up against in the present organization and racial constituency of the so-called German people; and I was equally surprised to find that practically nothing had been written on the ethnology or anthropology of the war.*
>
> *Shortly after America entered the war, I began giving, now and then, a lecture entitled "Long Heads and Round Heads, or What's the Matter with Germany." ... I believe that it is only intelligent patriotism that can develop determined patriots. I am therefore very much in earnest in my propaganda of spreading this teaching broadcast, and it is just a part of my enthusiasm to get these facts before as large a number of our people. I have found this presentation of the war very helpful to a large group of our troubled and perplexed citizenship; and it has also been helpful in getting certain groups of our foreign born citizens to better understand present problems.*[306]

---

[305] Christy Interview.
[306] Unpublished letter from William S. Sadler to Harry P. Harrison, March 18, 1918, Talent file, Redpath Collection.

The Secretary of State heard Sadler deliver this lecture in the East and asked him how long it would take him to write a book on this subject. Sadler replied that if he had a weekend he should be able to dictate it into book form. This lecture was published and later received honorable mention from the French government. Sadler became attached to the National Council of Defense, a war department bureau, as a lecturer.[307] During the war years he presented this lecture to thousands of persons with "no other thought than that it shall help my fellow - Americans better to understand the present conflict and, therefore, better to do their duty as American citizens in this trying hour." [308]

The first quarter of the twentieth century saw many changes in the status, behavior and attitudes of American women. Before World War I, American women were trying to create laws to stop prostitution, to bring about prohibition and in general to raise men's standards of living to their own. However, after World War I, many women forgot about changing the standards of the opposite sex and concentrated on new life styles for themselves. Women began to appear in the "speakeasies" and the new cocktail bars. The "flappers," the mod woman of the post war period, not only changed her attitudes concerning the drinking of alcoholic beverages but frequently adopted *avant - garde* attitudes concerning the hemline, courtship, sex, and companionate marriages.[309]

The "dance craze" with its excitement about ragtime became

---

[307] Christy Sadler, Personal correspondence between Dr. Sadler's daughter and the writer, November 4, 1969 and February 3, 1970. Also, Sprunger Interview.

[308] Sadler, Long Heads and Round Heads, pp. vii - viii.

[309] George Edwin Mowry, *The Twenties: Ford's Flappers and Fanatics* (Englewood Cliffs, N. J.: Prentice - Hall, 1963), p. 173. Hereafter cited as Mowry, *The Twenties*.

associated with a wave of sensualism and indecency.[310] "The new dances were denounced in press and pulpit, prohibited or carefully restricted in the colleges (Columbia specified six inches between dancers)."[311]

During this same period the popular press was presenting Sigmund Freud as a wizard, suggesting that he was a surgeon of the soul "who had a secret formula for ending mental disease and restoring social efficiency overnight, that is, for casting out devils."[312]

> In certain Chicago and New York circles before the war Freudian jargon was compulsory, everybody's friends were being "done," and already references to dreams or slips of the tongue gave rise to knowing winks.[313]

Not all institutions and individuals shared the enthusiasm of the emancipated woman. In some situations the popular topics of the day were placed on the taboo list:

> Upsetting plans for the feature number of the Chautauqua course being held on the Morningside College Campus under community auspices, officials of the college today compelled the show leaders to dispense with a scheduled debate tonight on companionate marriage. The college heads declared there is only one side to the subject of companionate marriage and therefore it is undebatable.[314]

The Board of Temperance, Prohibition, and Morals of the

---

[310] Henry F. May, The End of American Innocence: A Study of the First Years of Our Times, 1912 - 1917 (New York: Knopf, 1959), pp. 338 - 339. Hereafter cited as May, End of American Innocence.
[311] Ibid.
[312] May, *End of American Innocence*, p. 235. pp. 338 - 339.
[313] Ibid, pp. 338-339
[314] *The American Mercury*, September, 1928, p. 29.

Methodist Episcopal Church, in 1919, reported that the "increased use of tobacco smoking among women... was appalling" and made an "earnest appeal to women to refrain from the use of tobacco in the name of the country's welfare."[315]

It was during this period that Sadler prepared a special lecture for female audiences. Entitled "Personality and Health," it became a popular speech which presented an appreciation of woman's rights and her new freedom while at the same time extolling the merits of careful attention to the dangers of an over zealous use of that freedom. Discussing such relevant topics as "discretion," "modesty," "temperance," and "self-control," this lecture was a classical adaptation to the female mood of the times:

> I imagine there is little need for me to raise my voice here in protest against the use of alcohol and tobacco ... I haven't a word to say. I don't question that you have an equal right with men to become drunkards or cigarette fiends. I think that is just as much your right as is the right to vote, but it doesn't make it morally or ethically right, even if it is politically right.[316]

Historians could not keep from eyeing the new fad of clothing:

> The costumes of 1914 seemed to some the last word in indecency. The ideal conception of American womanhood could hardly survive the hobble skirt, the transparent waist, the increase in the use of cosmetics, the decline of the corset, let alone the degeneration of manners.[317]

---

[315] Reprint from *New York Times*, February 29, 1929, in Mowry, *The Twenties*.
[316] Sadler, *Personality and Health*, pp. 111 - 112. (This speech was stenographically reported as given to his audience.)
[317] May, *End of American Innocence*, p. 339.

Sadler easily adapted to his audiences of women concerning the new style in dress as he believed in their ideas:

> *I am often asked as a physician, what my opinion is as to the effect of the short dress, which has been in vogue in recent years, upon the morals of the country. I don't see any bad effects to be charged up to the short skirt. I think the young men who grow up during such fashions, perhaps will be possessed of less sex curiosity than those who grew up on a period of long skirt fashions.*[318]

Sadler must have appealed to his women auditors as he used a primary motive to build their self - esteem, and to inform them that they "one - upped the men."

> *I think, on the whole, women are to be congratulated for the large number of commonsense practices that have come into fashion in the past ten years, as regards their clothing. I think in some respects you have made more progress than we men have, who still wear our stiff collars and cling to other foolish habits of dress; whereas a dozen years ago we used to make fun of your wasp waists, trailing skirts, etc.*[319]

---

[318] Sadler, Personality and Health, p. 56.
[319] Ibid, p. 55.

V. THE SPEECH

Many important and historically significant speeches of the past have been lost to the speech critic simply because they were not put into print. In some cases this can only be construed as a major deficit in the accounts of human record keeping. In other cases, the absence of available transcripts may very well be a providential legacy. Chautauqua audiences were not always satisfied with the lectures delivered before them and frequently found sufficient reason to complain concerning their quality and their appropriateness. Managers of chautauqua circuits, attuned to the economic value of a satisfied audience, realized that just any man with a lecture would not be a successful addition to their programs. "Because one man makes a decided success in one line of lecturing is not proof that a dozen others can do the same."[320]

It is an attestation to the reception accorded the lectures of Dr. Sadler that many requests were made for copies of his lectures. In response to these requests, numerous texts of his lectures found their way into print; two of them from stenographic records made of actual lectures.

The choice of one of these speeches, "What a Salesman Should Know About His Health," as a subject for evaluation and criticism in this chapter was made for the following reasons:

1. It is a representative speech. Not only does it represent the health theme of other lectures, but it contains many of the same ideas, illustrations, and emphases as can be found in other presentations.

---

[320] Kennedy, *Yearbook*.

2. This speech was stenographically reported. The text goes so far as to include notations of applause.

3. This speech had wide distribution. In addition to the occasions when it was offered to special Chautauqua audiences, it was presented before conventions of sales and executive forces from such organizations as: The United States Rubber Company, the United States Tire Company, Universal Portland Cement Company, Illinois Manufacturers' Association, Chicago Chamber of Commerce, Michigan Manufacturers' Association, the Traffic Club of Chicago, the Packinghouse Sales Convention, Libby, McNeill & Libby, Swift & Company, plus various Rotary clubs and metropolitan Chambers of Commerce, Burroughs Adding Machine Company, National Warehousemen's Associations, and others.[321]

The popularity of lectures dealing with success in business careers was considerable during the first three decades of this century. In 1912, Dale Carnegie had offered his first course designed to build confidence. Chautauqua audiences, according to Edna Erie Wilson, appreciated the same theme. She wrote, in 1923, "... and once assembled, the audience will sit for an hour and a half under a tent with the mercury steadily mounting and listen, without even fanning, to a serious discourse upon how to succeed in business.[322]

Dispositio

The classical rhetoricians believed that effective organization was essential in a speech. They designated *dispositio* to deal with the selection, orderly arrangement, and proportion of the parts of a speech.[323]

---

[321] Sadler, *What a Salesman Should Know about his Health*, publisher's preface.
[322] Wilson, "Amusement a La Carte," p. 30.
[323] Thonssen and Baird, *Speech Criticism*, p. 392.

The rhetorical *dispositio* of Sadler's speech followed the tripartite division. It was the contention of Plato that:

> ... every speech ought to be put together like a living creature, with a body of its own, so as to be neither without head, nor without feet, but to have both a middle and extremities, described proportionately to each other and to the whole.[324]

His arrangement in the exordium was economical; approximately fifteen minutes was used in this introduction. This brevity might be juxtaposed with the speech in its entirety which did not terminate for two or two and one - half hours after the exordium. Although a speech of this length would be regarded excessively tiresome today, Chautauqua audiences were quite accustomed to lectures of several hours in length. Sadler followed Quintilian's concepts in the introduction: he secured his audience's good will by telling them that he had earned his medical education by selling, and he gave many personal illustrations concerning his days as a salesman. This was a feasible format for him to use in order to create a common bond with the salesmen. Dr. Sadler used a motto, "DO IT NOW" as an attention - getting device; he prepared his auditors for the purpose of his speech by using an illustration of an executive who came to his office for consultation. The executive cured himself by adopting Sadler's advice concerning working and living.

In a consistent and logical transition between the introduction and the discussion the three main divisions of the speech are presented lucidly.

---

[324] Henry Cary (trans.), *Phaedrus; The Works of Plato*, I (London: J.M. Dent and Sons, Ltd., 1854), 342 - 343.

First: I want to talk to you about personality, the pep machine that is to do the work; the mind and the body unite into that structure which we commonly know by the names of character, or personality. Under this head we will consider the mental elements of a successful business career.

Second: I want to talk about health, the actual energy, the steam which we must have to drive this personality engine down the highway of success and achievement. Under this head we will discuss the physical elements or factors making for success in business.

Third: I want to discuss with you the true and false safety valves for pep, which must be a part of the equipment of every personality machine in its successful battle for material advancement and business success.[325]

The internal composition of Sadler's speech was composed with the awareness of the needs of his audience; the selection of supporting materials, the elimination of medical jargon, the colorful metaphors, the trite clichés and maxims had appeal for the audience of his day. This speech was for a man in the field of business, a salesman, the illustrations were applicable to the life of a salesman; the stories were about experiences of salesmen.

In the first main idea concerning the topic of mental elements, seven supporting proofs were developed. The development of this idea was exhaustive enough to be a complete speech today. Understanding that an audience's attention span was short, Sadler purposely used *digressio* and a variety of attention - getting devices in his discussion. Speaking of the "ductless gland

---

[325] Sadler, *Salesman*, p. 16.

theory of personality," he offered expert medical opinions, supported with factual examples and illustrations, metaphorical illustrations, specific instances and maxims. His discussion was arranged so that the audience could understand it, while the maxims and clichés acted as mnemonic devices to help them remember and retain the information. Sadler demonstrated the artistic technique of adapting his ideas to their level of comprehension and interest. It was Sadler's belief that an auditor's attention span was a maximum of five to six minutes.[326]

Sadler followed the belief of Quintilian concerning the use of humor; his entire speech sparkled with a display of wit and comic tension release. Quintilian advocated the use of humor:

> *I now turn to a very different talent, namely that which dispels the graver emotions of the judge by exciting his laughter, frequently diverts his attention from the facts of the case, and sometimes even refreshes him and revives him when he has begun to be bored or wearied by the case.*[327]
>
> *Now, though laughter may be regarded as a trivial matter it has a certain imperious force of its own which it is very hard to resist.*[328]

The classical authorities all agreed to the importance of using the proper strategical methods in the peroration or conclusion of a speech. W. N. Brigance concurred:

> *Now the condition which confronts a speaker in closing his speech is this: His last words must leave the strongest possible emotional impression; they must lead the*

---

[326] Christy Interview.
[327] H. E. Butler (trans.), *The Institutio Oratoria of Quintilian*, Book VI. lii. 1. Hereafter cited as Butler, *Quintilian*.
[328] Ibid, p. 8.

> *audience to feel the justice or righteousness of the speaker's cause; they must, if possible, make the audience want to believe or act.... A summary which reaches the intellect alone is not sufficient. It must also reach the emotions.*[329]

> *We must remember that if the speaker expects the audience to change its belief or to go forth and act upon his words, he must leave them in a favorable state of mind. Cold logic is not enough. We may talk all we please about people being moved by logic only - but it will all be just talk, for people are not moved by cold reasoning alone. I do not mean to say that people are not influenced by reason, but rather that they are not influenced by reason alone - that we are also influenced by our likes and dislikes, our loves and our fears, our pocketbooks and our pride - and that our actions are a result of the interaction of our emotions and our reasoning (if these can ever be purely separate) with the balance of the ledger on the side of our emotions.*[330]

Although the peroration to this speech was surprisingly brief, it should be noted that Sadler made brief summations of points presented in the text of the address itself. The conclusion, nevertheless, follows the instruction of classical theory. According to Aristotle, four emphases ought to appear in the epilogue:

> *(1) You must render the audience well - disposed to yourself; (2) You must magnify and depreciate; (3) you must put the audience into the right state of emotion; and (4) you must refresh their memories.*[331]

Sadler appears to have accomplished this, although the first

---

[329] William Norwood Brigance, *The Spoken Word* (New York: F. S. Crofts and Co., 1929), p. 107. Hereafter cited as Brigance, *Word*.
[330] Brigance, *Word*, p. 106.
[331] Lane Cooper (trans.), *The Rhetoric of Aristotle* (New York: D. Appleton and Company, 1932), 3. 19. Hereafter cited as *The Rhetoric of Aristotle*.

emphasis is indirectly presented by reliance upon his character and the use of the first person pronouns:

> Gentlemen, I have told you of better safety valves for your excess animal spirits. I have described to you saner and safer outlets for your excess pep; and I am going to believe that you are going to follow this advice, and that you are going to shun these questionable and vicious channels of self - expression; that you are going to find saner and more self - respecting methods for having fun. Let us enroll ourselves in the cause of better thinking, higher living; let us become apostles of a new evangelism, of honest business, healthful habits, clear thinking, and clean living. I thank you.[332]

The concluding remarks appear to have also met the criteria for organization set down by W. N. Brigance.

Electio

Buffon made an insightful summation when he said, *"Le style c'est l'hornme meme."*[333] Murry stated: "Style is the direct expression of an individual mode of experience."[334] The ancient rhetoricians used the terms *electio* or *elecutio* to designate style. Quintilian set forth the importance of style when he said:

It is a great gift to be able to set forth the facts on which we are speaking clearly and vividly. For oratory fails of its full effect, and does not assert itself as it should if its appeal is merely to the hearing.... one form of vividness which consists in giving

---

[332] Sadler, *Salesman*, pp. 126 - 127.
[333] Robert T. Oliver, "Oratory of Burke, Fox, Sheridan, and Pitt" (unpublished Doctor's dissertation, University of Wisconsin, 1937), pp. 87 - 88.
[334] Middleton Murry, *The Problem of Style* (London: Oxford University Press, 1922), pp. 3 - 8.

an actual word - picture of a scene.³³⁵

It was Sadler's style: his manner, word choice, tonality, clearness, usage, patterns of communication, sincerity, personality and total manner of presenting information that made him a popular lecturer.

> Last evening after being introduced by Dr. Busse, representing the local medical society, Dr. Sadler gave one of his unique lectures which vitally interested everybody and no lecturer who ever appeared at this Chautauqua was ever given better attention.³³⁶

An objective scientific analysis of style as a tool is limited to the oral arrangement of the intangible words of the sender, and to the understanding and the interpretation of the words involved when one tries to qualify the style of a speaker. Every word that a speaker uses is a symbol of his emotional, cultural and experiential level. The receiver interprets these words in the symbols of his personal, unique, emotional, cultural and experiential field. Thus, it would appear that the most feasible analysis should be a quantitative one since the technique of the speaker in the use of words and in the arrangement of the words remains fairly constant.

a physician noted as an eloquent orator, Cicero argued that Asclepiades:

> . . . at the time when he was surpassing the rest of his profession in eloquence, [he] was exhibiting, in such graceful speaking, the skill of an orator, not that of a physician. ³³⁷

---

³³⁵ Butler, *Quintilian*, VIII. 111. 62 - 63.
³³⁶ The Courier Newspaper, Madison, Indiana, p. 18, in Sadler, Popular Health Lectures.
³³⁷ Cicero De Oratore, I. xiv. 62

... it is nearer the truth to say that neither can anyone be eloquent upon a subject that is unknown to him, nor, if he knows it perfectly and yet does not know how to shape and polish his style, can he speak fluently even upon that which he does know. [338]

Sadler used a motivating technique of style in the beginning of his speech as he gave his audience a slogan, "DO IT NOW." He revealed his own philosophy of life as he told his audience:

> *If you ever come to my office you will find the top of my desk usually empty except for an ink well and a pen ... you will find even the middle drawer, in which I keep my unfinished business, usually empty. I am all the time meeting business men who have their brains jammed so full of unfinished business, unsettled problems, that they are not only falling down in the selling game, but they are ruining their health.* [340]

Sadler's medical lectures gave the Chautauqua audience the latest information that medical science could contribute toward making them healthy individuals. It is an artistic accomplishment when a speaker has the ability to use ornament in a prosaic, informative topic concerned with heredity, blood pressure, adequate elimination, muscular exercise, and disease.

---

[338] Ibid, I. xiv. 63.
[339] Ref. Image: anmpx09x0102, Asclepiade / Asclepiades / Asclepius
Author of the picture: Forestier
Technique: Engraving.
(http://www.biusante.parisdescartes.fr/histmed/image?anmpx09x0102)
[340] Sadler, *Salesman*, p. 15.

The topical order was employed; he was meticulous in his use of transitions to link each topic with the ones preceding and following it. Each topic was handled with ease, taste and fluency.

Continuing his treatment of style, Cicero wrote:

> ... in the general structure of the language, after we have mastered smoothness of arrangement and the principle of rhythm that I spoke of, we then must vary and intersperse all our discourse with brilliant touches both of thought and of language.[341]

Sadler followed Cicero's teaching on oratory; he knew the response that he desired in an audience, thus, he presented the necessary stimulus in order to initiate this response. The metaphor and the allegory were used to underscore salient points not only as restatements of the medical advice given, but as "brilliant touches" to adorn.

> Nature is a good book - keeper and though your ancestors may have endowed you with good vital resistance, if you abuse your health sooner or later Old Mother Nature will meet you around the corner with a stuffed club and you will have a sudden jolt, a rude awakening.[342]

> . . . fear is the salesman's assassin. Fear is the thing that can steal into the salesman's mind, creep up over his ambition, and before it gets through have him bound hand and foot -- hog tied -- while it laughs in the face of his consternation fear is a heartless, cold - blooded, psychologic monstrosity that, when once it lays its fiendish hand on the throat of an otherwise successful salesman,

---

[341] Cicero De Oratore, III. lii, 201.
[342] Sadler, *Salesman*, p. 69.

> *never loosens its grip until it has brought him down in ruination and failure ...* [343]

Sadler employed a simple but effective device to enliven his lecture and to maintain the attention of his audience. After each statement of factual medical information, relevant supporting statements in the form of examples, illustrations, maxims, or clichés were injected. Occasionally, a touch of dialect served the purpose. Cicero would have agreed with this procedure because he believed in a

> *... digression from the matter at issue; and after this has supplied entertainment the return to the subject will have to be neatly and tactfully effected; and its distinction from what has already been said; ... or saying one thing and meaning another, which has a very great influence on the minds of the audience, and which is extremely entertaining if carried on in a conversational and not a declamatory tone; ...* [344]

Sadler's tropes were not only attention - getting devices, but they filled his prose with color. "The successful salesman must be an individual who can 'think like greased lightning' and make up his mind with the 'velocity of a western cyclone.'"[345] Sadler predicted what experience will do for the salesman; "it will enable him to drink water that someone else has pumped"[346] or through experience the salesman "learns how to set his sails with a favoring wind and to sleep and rest up in a time of calm."[347] As Sadler discussed elimination, he said, "... every time you eat a meal, swallow a broom with the meal to sweep it out."[348] As he talked of common diseases he said, "...

---

[343] Ibid, p. 40.
[344] Cicero De Oratore, III. liii. 203.
[345] Sadler, *Salesman*, p. 19.
[346] Sadler, *Salesman*, p. 45.
[347] Ibid.
[348] Ibid, p.93.

those little foxes which nibble at the vines of health so insidiously;[349] ... these little fellows [cells] when they are bathed with this nourishing non-irritating blood, begin to feel like a million dollars."[350]

Sadler avoided pedantry; he had a conversational plain style of speaking and used perspicuous terminology when discussing psychiatry with a lay audience. This doctor who had a large vocabulary of exclusive medical terms at his disposal followed Cicero's belief that one should speak in a common manner.

> ... for the vocabulary of conversation is the same as that of formal oratory, and we do not choose one class of words for daily use and another for full-dress public occasions, but we pick them up from common life as they lie at our disposal and then shape them and mold them at our discretion, like the softest wax. Consequently at one moment we use a dignified style, at another a plain one, and at another we keep a middle course between the two; thus the style of our oratory follows the line of thought we take, and changes and turns to suit all the requirements of pleasing the ear and influencing the mind of the audience.[351]

According to the Flesch formula for readability based on the number of syllables, words and sentences found in selected samples of this speech, Sadler is rated fairly difficult. The average plane of this speech is best suited to an audience with a tenth or twelfth grade education. It appeared that he always considered his audience and tried to adapt to them. The press opinion of *The Journal* in Racine, Wisconsin said during one of his Chautauqua lectures, "[Dr. Sadler] drew one of the largest audiences of the week. The lecture was sane, sensible, inspiring

---

[349] Ibid, p.27.
[350] Ibid, p. 81.
[351] *Cicero De Oratore*, III. xlv. 177.

and helpful."³⁵²

Cicero believed that an orator should speak in the language of his auditor:

> ... the word may either be archaic but at the same time acceptable to habitual usage; or a coinage made by compounding two words, or inventing a new one -- and here similarly consideration must be paid to what our ears are used to; or used metaphorically -- a most effective way of introducing spots of high light to give brilliance to the style.³⁵³

Sadler often used clichés and maxims to illustrate a point; terms such as "milk of human kindness,"³⁵⁴ "friendly human touch,"³⁵⁵ "cottoning up,"³⁵⁶ to you, are found in all of his speeches. He would tell his audience to "cultivate horse-sense,"³⁵⁷ "come down off your high horse,"³⁵⁸ and "cut out the booze."³⁵⁹ His maxims were enthymematic. "You can fool some of your customers all the time and you can fool all of your customers some of the time."³⁶⁰ "Your competitor is always a 'lucky dog' while you think your luck is rotten."³⁶¹

Cicero believed that "... impersonation of people, an extremely brilliant method of amplification; picturing of results; putting on the wrong scent; raising a laugh"; was appealing to some

---

352 The Journal, Racine, Wisconsin, in Sadler, Popular Health Lectures.
353 *Cicero De Oratore*, III. xliii. 170.
354 Sadler, *Salesman*, p. 30.
355 Ibid, p. 37.
356 Ibid, p. 38.
357 Ibid, p. 42.
358 Ibid, p.111.
359 Ibid, p. 123.
360 Sadler, *Salesman*, p. 32.
361 Ibid, p.105

audiences.[362] Sadler tells his audience that he was teaching one of his Irish patients the proper way to breathe; when she finally understood she said, "Oh, now I understand. Shure you wan me to breathe just like a cow, from shtem to shtern."[363] He also used dialect as he suggested that his audience eat the solid part of their food. "Be like the little fellow who said to his playmate: 'There ain't gonna be no core to this apple.'" [364]

Sadler followed the oratory of Cicero, "No one should be numbered with the orators who is not accomplished in all those arts that befit the well - bred."[365] The manner in which he used the *bon mot* was epigramatic; some of his originals are still applicable and quotable today.

The magnetism of Sadler was revealed in his style; he knew how to "touch an audience." As people walked and drove home from his Chautauqua lecture, they must have continued to think of the many living examples and illustrations of how to maintain good health. His felicitous style had the quality of creating an indelible impression.

Inventio

Cicero believed that *inventio* [invention] was the Creative ability of the orator to "first hit upon what to say; then manage and marshal his discoveries, not merely in orderly fashion, but with a discriminating eye for the exact weight as it were of each argument; ..." [366]

Aristotle defined rhetoric, "as the faculty of discovering in the

---

[362] *Cicero De Oratore*, III. liii. 205.
[363] Sadler, *Salesman*, p. 57.
[364] Ibid.
[365] *Cicero De Oratore*, I. xvi. 72.
[366] *Cicero De Oratore*, I. xxxi. 142.

particular case what are the available means of persuasion."³⁶⁷ A speech has two types of proof or means of persuasion: the non-artistic and the artistic. The non-artistic proofs are those that were in existence, e.g., witnesses, laws, contracts, fortunes, and oaths. The artistic proofs are those that are created by the speaker, e.g., *ethos*, the character of the speaker; *pathos*, producing the proper emotional attitude in the audience; and *logos*, the source of persuasion based on the example and the enthymeme.³⁶⁸

Ethos

Cato's definition of an orator was, "A good man skilled in speaking."³⁶⁹ He explained this concept more specifically as he stated:

> *The ethos, of which we form a conception, and which we desire to find in speakers, is recommended, above all, by goodness, being not only mild and placid, but for the most part pleasing and polite, and amiable and attractive to the hearers; and the greatest merit in the expression of it, is, that it should seem to flow from the nature of the things and persons with which we are concerned so that the moral character of the speaker may clearly appear, and be recognized, as it were, in his discourse.³⁷⁰*

Plato believed that the truly eloquent orator was one who possessed *ethos;* he conceived this construct of *ethos* as being multifaceted: the speaker should possess good character;³⁷¹ the

---

³⁶⁷ The *Rhetoric of Aristotle*, 1.2 1355ᵇ
³⁶⁸ Ibid. 1.2 1355ᵇ-1356ᵃ
³⁶⁹ Butler, *Quintilian*, XII. 1. 44.
³⁷⁰ J. S. Watson (trans.), Quintilian's Institutes of *Oratory*, I, VI (London: G. Bell and Sons, 1913), 5. Hereafter cited as Watson, *Quintilian*.
³⁷¹ *Laws*, 601; *Phaedrus*, 270; and *Gorgias*, 500. Citations from the *Phaedrus*

speaker should be intelligent and informed;[372] the speaker should adapt his arguments to the audience;[373] speaker should consider the good will of the audience. [374]

During the twelve years Sadler spoke on the Chautauqua circuit, he established *ethos* extrinsically weeks or months before even arriving at the Chautauqua stop. His reputation, sagacity, and good will were anticipated through the circulation of brochures containing not only a handsome, professional picture of the coming lecturer, but also citations on his ethical authority plus reviews and comments from previous auditors:

> Dr. Sadler's lecture on Faith and Fear was the best thing yet produced on this platform, and we do not forget nor fail to appreciate Gunsaulus, Medbury, Seton and the rest.[375]

> At four o'clock the Sadlers [his wife accompanied him] condensed an entire Chautauqua, except the music, into two and a half hours, for the audience kept them at work until half - past six. In saving of life and in increased health and happiness this two and a half hours was worth the cost of the entire Chautauqua.[376]

Sadler established *ethos* by the technique of having the local doctor introduce him to the Chautauqua audience. As this home - town doctor with a local prestigious position literally placed his stamp of approval on Sadler, a subliminal, marginal

---

and *Gorgias* are based upon Lane Cooper's *Plato* (London: Oxford University Press, 1938). All other references are from the five volume, third edition of *Plato's Dialogues* by Benjamin- Jowett (Oxford: The Clarendon Press, 1392).

[372] *Lysis*, 210.
[373] *Phaedrus*, 270, 274.
[374] *Laws*, 722-723.
[375] Sadler, Popular Health Lectures.
[376] Ibid.

trust factor entered between him and his audience thus creating his credibility, and enhancing his prestige.

Sadler's character, intelligence, and good will were reiterated in the ethical implication in the introduction given by the home-town doctor.

> Dr. William S. Sadler, well - known surgeon, author and lecturer of Chicago is a professor at the Post - Graduate Medical School of Chicago, a director and, chief psychiatrist of the Chicago Institute of Research and Diagnosis, consulting psychiatrist at Columbus Hospital, consultant in psychiatry to the W. K. Kellogg Foundation.... The Doctor has written more than a score of books...... The Doctor is a Fellow of the American Medical Association, the American Psychiatric Association, and the American Association for the Advancement of Science. He is a member of the American Psychopathological Association, and numerous other allied medical societies and scientific bodies. [377]

Aristotle's *Poetics* states that since an orator is free to select his own topics and arguments, this serves as moral proof of his *ethos:* "Just as the orator selects arguments which reveal his character, so a character in a drama, through the way he argues *(dianoia)* shows his *ethos.*"[378]

The ethical element of the subject of his speech, "What Every Salesman Should Know About His Health," established good will in revealing genuine interest in the welfare of his audience. His purpose for speaking, "I propose to give you the latest information that medical science has to contribute toward

---

[377] Sadler's Papers.
[378] William Hamilton Fyfe (trans.), *Aristotle: Poetics* (London: W. Heinemann, Ltd., 1932), VI, 29.

making a salesman happy, healthy, and efficient,"[379] fulfills the self-preservation motive and lends itself to a willing belief and confidence in Sadler.

Isocrates revealed his concept of the importance of *ethos* in an orator as he said, "... the power to speak well is taken as the surest index of a sound understanding, and discourse which is true and lawful and just as the outward image of a good and faithful soul."[380]

During his speaking on the circuit, Sadler did not use notes;[381] this no-manuscript style not only added to his appearance and to his manner of delivery, but possibly to his credibility. If he had found it necessary to continually focus his eyes on a medical manuscript, the audience might have doubted his sagacity.

He revealed his good will and sincere interest in their welfare by answering the questions that he felt they might be inquisitive about.

> ... you may be more or less curious to know why I, a medical man, should be asked to come here and talk to you on the elements of successful salesmanship ... because first, as you shall presently see, good health is the real foundation of the essential elements of pep.[382]

> ... I am probably here talking to you salesmen on personality and pep because of the fact that I have had considerable experience as a salesman, and therefore I talk to you in the light of that experience and in the language of tile salesman .... part of the money I used to

---

[379] Sadler, *Salesman,* p. 9.
[380] George Norlin (trans.), *Isocrates: Antidosis* (London: W. Heinemann, Ltd., 1929), II, 255.
[381] Christy Interview.
[382] Ibid, p. 11.

> *obtain my medical education and acquire my present status I earned as a traveling salesman.*[383]

Cicero believed that in order to be a genuine orator, one must have some knowledge of all subject matter; he felt that an orator must understand the life of mankind.

> *For the genuine orator must have investigated and heard and read and discussed and handled and debated the whole of the contents of the life of mankind, inasmuch as that is the field of the orator's activity, the subject matter of his study.*[384]

Obviously, Sadler understood the orientation of the salesmen. Empathy for the salesman's life - style was the base on which Sadler projected his concern for their well - being.

> *I know what this "selling game" is -- every step of it -- every pitfall, and every slippery place in the game, from the time you say "Good morning," and shake hands with your prospect, until you succeed or fail to get his name on the dotted line.*[385]

Sadler obviously strove to establish an intimate and friendly relationship with his listeners; Quintilian would have recommended him as being an effective teacher: "... it is further of the very first importance, that he should be on friendly and intimate terms with us and make his teaching not a duty but a labour of love."[386]

Sadler conformed to the *mores civitatis* of his auditors by revealing that he was one of them.

---

[383] Sadler, *Salesman*, p. 10.
[384] *Cicero De Orators*, III. xiv. 54.
[385] Sadler, *Salesman*, p. 12.
[386] Butler, *Quintilian*, I. 11. 15.

> *I have been up and down the length and breadth of this land; I know about life on the road; I understand all about getting out on a "Blue Monday" morning when business is "rotten," and trying to sell goods to a man whom my competitor has already oversold.* [387]

Laughter and witticism can be equated with *ethos*. Cicero believed that jesting had rhetorical appropriateness: "... merriment naturally wins goodwill for its author; and everyone admires acuteness ... it shows the orator himself to be a man of finish, accomplishment and taste."[388]

When Sadler was telling his audience that play rejuvenated one after work wears them out, he suggested that they find a "fad" or a "hobby." The artistic proof of *ethos* was evident in his feeling of good will toward them as he cited the personal reason for giving the speech.

> *This thing is a sort of hobby with me, it is a fad ... I'm having the time of my life up here... You may be working down there listening to me, I hope not too hard, but I am playing up here while I am talking to you on salesmanship.* [389]

Throughout his speech, Sadler continually associated the goals of his discourse with what was virtuous, right and good. Ralph Waldo Emerson defined eloquence as "the art of speaking what you mean and are," and called this art the "authentic sign."[390] Sadler revealed himself and his character in the advice: "... we must be able to show an interest in the other fellow."[391] "You must have confidence in your firm." "You must be loyal

---

[387] Sadler, *Salesman*, p. 11.
[388] *Cicero De Oratore*, II. lviii. 236.
[389] *Cicero De Oratore*, II. lviii. 236.
[390] Thonssen and Baird, *Speech Criticism*, p. 383.
[391] Sadler, *Salesman*, p. 32.

and have an enthusiastic spirit for teamwork." [392] "... master the art of living with yourself as you are and the world as it is."[393] "Don't knock your competitor -- study his methods..."[394]

Sadler's knowledge of human emotions and his concern for good will toward others led him to suggest: "... introduce yourself to the human race ... and you will find it a source of great delight and endless enjoyment."[395]

Aristotle called the artistic proofs the means of persuasion that a speaker must find and invent for himself. He affirmed that the speaker's character, namely *ethos*, was "the most potent of all the means to persuasion."[396] The artistic proof that produces the most impact in Sadler's speech is *ethos*. Throughout this speech he relied upon authority derived from his own experience in the medical field as he created a common bond with his audience. This man of intellectual integrity diffused the feeling with these particular listeners that he too had been exposed to their frustrations, known their temptations, experienced failure, but like them had also enjoyed the pleasure of success.

---

[392] Ibid, p. -38.
[393] Ibid, p. 42.
[394] Ibid, p. 46.
[395] Ibid, p. 112.
[396] The Rhetoric of Aristotle, 1.2. 1356 [a]

Pathos

"Persuasion," wrote Aristotle, "is effected through the audience when they are brought by the speech into a state of emotion."[397] For centuries man has tried to find a simple explanation of what motivates people to react as they do. Even though theorists have not found an all-encompassing hypothesis of what motivates individuals to act, they know that certain motive appeals assist in the understanding of human nature and of human behavior. Aristotle concluded that: "... we give very different decisions under the sway of pain or joy, and liking or hatred."[398]

> *The same thing does not appear the same to men when they are friendly and when they hate, nor when they are angry and when they are in a gentle mood; in these different moods the same thing will appear either wholly different in kind, or different as to magnitude.*[399]

It was Webster's belief that:

> *... violence of language was indicative of feebleness of thought and want of reasoning power, and it was his practice rather to understand than overstate the strength of his confidence in the soundness of his own arguments ... not by himself.*[400]

However, as Dr. Chauncey A. Goodrich observed Webster as he spoke in defense of his Alma Mater, Dartmouth College, Webster's "lips quivered; his firm cheeks trembled with emotion; his eyes were filled with tears, his voice choked, and he

---

[397] Ibid.
[398] Ibid.
[399] *The Rhetoric of Aristotle*, 1377ᵇ, 1378ᵃ
[400] George Perkins Marsh, *Lectures on the English Language* (New York: Scribner, 1863), p. 235.

seemed struggling to the utmost simply to gain that mastery over himself." Dr. Goodrich noted, "one thing it taught me, that the pathetic depends not merely on the words uttered, but still more on the estimate we put upon him who utters them."[401] Sadler depended on the pathetic appeal to demonstrate the truth of the immediateness of his health message to the salesmen.

Sadler's introduction he presents a dichotomy of both ethical and emotional appeal as he tells his audience that he is not going to give a prosaic medical lecture as they would expect a doctor to give, but he is going to talk to them in a language that is easily understood.

In Campbell's analysis of circumstances which were operational on passions, he believed that the most powerful was that of interest.[402]

> ... a person present with us, whom we see and hear, and who, by words, and looks, and gestures, gives the liveliest signs of his feelings, has the surest and most immediate claim upon our sympathy. We become infected with his passions. We are hurried along by them, and not allowed leisure to distinguish between his relation and our relation, his interest and our interest.[403]

The appeal to self - preservation was utilized as a primary motive appeal as Sadler sought to enlist concern and inspire action in his audience of salesmen. This powerful motive was given serious as well as humorous reinforcement.

---

[401] The account of the scene was procured from Dr. Goodrich by Rutus Choate for his memorial address on Webster at Dartmouth College, 1853. It is quoted in full in Benjamin Franklin Tefft, *Webster and His Masterpieces* (Buffalo: Orton and Mulligan, 1854), p. 187 sqq.
[402] Sadler, *Salesman*, p. 9.
[403] William P. Sanford, *English Theories of Public Address, 1530 - 1828* (Columbus, Ohio: Harold L. Hedrick, 1931), p. 146.

> ... as a physician I am interested in keeping you on earth as long as possible, in the harness, active, efficient and happy. I want to see you live healthful and useful lives while you are here, and to have you remain here your three score years and ten, or longer -- that you come nearer the ideal age of man, the century mark.[404]

Dr. Sadler firmly believed that according to the research he had done man should live to be one hundred years old.[405] He amplifies his attitude concerning longevity by using an illustration of a man who died prematurely. St. Peter had a difficult time finding the deceased man's name on the list; when he found it at the bottom, St. Peter said:

> "Why man you're not due up here for twenty years yet. Who was your doctor?"[406]

As the audience of businessmen listened, they were reminded of the health potentials which they possessed, of the ways in which men frequently abused these potentials and in familiar language found themselves being cajoled into positive practices for the preservation of health. Sadler reiterated this theme embellishing it with additional, personal illustrations and observations.

According to the instruction of Genung, Sadler employed the proper language:

> ... the speaker has to consult wisely the taste, the culture, the familiar ideas, of the persons addressed.... Uneducated people are more easily swayed by pathos, humor, or impassioned phrase; but at the same time

---

[404] Sadler, *Salesman*, p. 51.
[405] Ibid, p. 50.
[406] Sadler, *Salesman*, p. 52.

> *more palpable and striking, more coarse - grained means must be used ...*[407]

By identifying himself with the salesman, Sadler was able to combine pathetic and ethical appeals. As an example, when asserting the importance of sufficient sleep as being conducive to alertness, Sadler recalled:

> *Many are the times I can remember sitting around a hotel office to take a midnight train, or one at half - past one a.m., and all the while a bunch of traveling men are sitting around the lobby playing poker, in an atmosphere of tobacco smoke so dense you can hardly see through it.*[408]

Again the audience must have recognized the appeal to sensible eating habits when Sadler pointed out:

> *Remember, there are a lot of good American people digging their graves with their teeth. They sit down at the table three times a day and stuff food into their stomachs until the pain is greater at the equator than the pleasure at the north pole.*[409]

Resorting to medical theory, Sadler then particularized the types of individuals apt to be found in the field of sales. To each type he offered insights and advice. Characteristically, this emphasis promotes the recurrent theme of self - adjustment and self - actualization, both of which fall into the category of pathetic appeals.

---

[407] John Franklin Genung, The *Working Principles of Rhetoric* (New York: Ginn and Company, 1910), p. 655. Hereafter cited as Genung, *Principles*.
[408] Sadler, *Salesman*, p. 64.
[409] Sadler, *Salesman*, p. 63.

> The thyroid - dominant man is a natural pep machine. He just naturally feels peppy because his thyroid literally determines the rate at which energy is liberated in his body. On the other hand, the sub - thyroid man simply cannot whip himself into an exhibition of energy. He is inherently deficient in that thing which we call "Get up and get." Of course this super - thyroid man must watch his step. He is in danger of over-doing, he is in danger of breaking down, blowing up, or burning out.[410]

Sadler instructed his auditors that the thyroid - dominant man with his pep might be a better salesman, but the sub - thyroid man who is lacking some of this energy will possibly live the longest.

Cicero gave his views concerning emotional appeal: "[To] kindle the feelings of his hearers, or quench them when kindled ... it is in this that the orator's virtue and range are chiefly discerned."[411]

Sadler continued to appeal to the salesman's pride, honor, duty, reputation, and competitive nature as he explained that it was not always their fault should they not achieve great success.

> One salesman may be a howling success because his ductless glands are working just right -- or maybe over - secreting a trifle; another salesman works hard, meets with mediocre success, and in the end turns out a dismal failure just because his ductless glands fall down on him, they wouldn't stand up under the strain, they couldn't deliver the goods when he went up against the difficulties and worries of the selling game.[412]

Appealing to the energetic salesman as well as to the listless

---

[410] Ibid, p. 95.
[411] Cicero De Oratore, I. li. 219.
[412] Sadler, *Salesman*, p. 23.

salesman, he helped them to understand that hereditary conditions contributed to their chemistry make - up and thus endowed them with varying degrees of energy. Sadler fulfilled their esteem need of hope, desire and knowledge when he humorously related:

> Now, don't come to me after this lecture and ask me to shoot some of this success stuff into your veins with a hypodermic needle, to make you super - salesmen, because I can't do it; we haven't got that far -- at least, not yet -- but there's no telling but that some of you lame ducks get along better in the game.[413]

Genung believed that the appeal to the emotions could be compared to the working of the machine in getting the wheels in motion. "Once rouse the man to feel the issue, and the way is clear to translate enthusiasm into duty."[414]

This emphasis was also found in the writings of William James:

> If one must have a single name for the condition upon which the impulsive and inhibitive quality of objects depends, one had better call it their interest. "The interesting" is a title which covers not only the pleasant and the painful, but also the morbidly fascinating, the tediously haunting, and even the simple habitual, inasmuch as the attention usually travels on habitual lines, and what-we-attend-to and what-interests-us are synonymous terms.[415]

William James and John Dewey often stated in their works that the desire to be important and the craving to be appreciated constituted the deepest urges in human nature. Sigmund Freud believed that the most dynamic drives were the sex drives and

---

[413] Ibid., p. 29.
[414] Genung, *Principles*, p. 654.
[415] *Psychology, Briefer Course*, p. 448; in Brigance, *Word*.

the desire to be important. Sadler used the appeal of self - esteem; he gave his audience a feeling of personal worth; he knew that the salesmen listening to him had a desire to be somebody, a desire to be important in their own little world.

> *I am lecturing to go-getters, real live-wire salesmen. I hope I will always know how to be a good loser, to know when I'm licked, to get up and shake the dust off my feet, cry "Never touched me," and go into the game again. But I'll be blamed if I give up before they whip me - if I let the undertaker bury me before the doctor gets through with me.*[416]

In essence, Maslow's words, "What a man *can* be, he *must* be,"[417] through self-realization or actualization. This need can become so urgent that a person might willingly sacrifice health, love, and safety. Sadler gave his audience of salesmen hope when he told them that the opportunity of self - realization was open to them.

> *I know a very successful salesman, another patient of mine, who was told by one of the best men in the city of Chicago, presiding over a sales department, that he could never make a salesman. He got mad, gave the fellow a good cussing to his face, resigned, went out and got a job with the firm's most bitter competitor and today is their banner salesman - the man they send out to get the big orders and to break into a difficult field.*[418]

Sadler helped to fulfill his listeners' love for adventure in self-actualization as he nurtured their ego, and urged them to:

> *... hitch your wagon to a star, throw down the gauntlet, accept the gage of battle and go into it to win - all the while learning to be a good loser in all of the little minor*

---

[416] Sadler, *Salesman*, p. 34.
[417] A. H. Maslow, "A Theory of Human Motivation," *Psychological Review*, L (March, 1943), 382.
[418] Sadler, *Salesman*, p. 21.

> *defeats that must come to us as we play this interesting game, this game of life, this game of double stakes - success in the material struggle, success in the achievement of laurels in our day and generation.*[419]

Sadler continued to use the powerful effect of *pathos* as he continued to guide them toward the fulfillment of their potential -- self - realization.

> *I have known many a good salesman to fail because he was not able sufficiently to overcome his reticence, hesitancy, backwardness, indecision, and bashfulness ... I am talking about that whole - souled earnestness that characterized the young salesman who, when he had sneaked past the bodyguards and got into the Old Man's private office, never heard him when he ordered him out -- stayed right by the job and sold him ten carloads of merchandise.*[420]

"Emotion," wrote Genung, "... must exit in genuine depth and fullness in the orator himself, and flow to his hearers by the natural channel of truth."[421] Referring to the demands of his medical practice, Sadler told them that even though he would often be called in the middle of the night to see a patient, he still liked his job. He told the salesmen that they must be happy and contented in their positions in order to maintain good health.

Sadler, as a psychiatrist, knew the importance of personal enjoyment for sustaining mental health. He appealed to the need for recreation and pleasure and counseled:

---

[419] Ibid, p. 42.
[420] Ibid., p. 30.
[421] Genung, *Principles,* p. 656.

> *Children love to play, and they don't often have nervous prostration. We don't send businessmen off to sanitariums because they are "nutty" or brain - cracked, until they quit playing. We don't have to see the doctor about nerve exhaustion and brain fag until we have pursued our business activities to the neglect of our play life.*[422]

Patriotism to one's country or to one's place of business, loyalty to friends and family can give contentment to one's mental health. Sadler used this appeal as he suggested that a salesman must be happy in his business relationships or he should leave the firm and find a new position.

> *Loyalty breeds enthusiasm, it enlarges the horizon, it rests the nerves, it lightens the task, and eases the burden. Congenial business associates, agreeable commercial companions, turn work that would otherwise be drudgery into joy and delight.*[423]

Sadler reiterated the fact that it was imperative to believe in oneself if one wanted others to believe in him. He illustrated this idea with a humorous and nonsensical verse. He told his salesmen that in order to be effective, they must advertise themselves always. He referred them to a sign posted over a gasoline station that portrayed eternal advertising.

Day by day in every way
Our service is better and better;
Our water is wetter and wetter;
Our oil is slicker and slicker;
Our gas fires quicker and quicker.[424]

The significance of the pathetic appeal in oratory revolves

---

[422] Sadler, *Salesman*, p. 106.
[423] Ibid, p. 104.
[424] Sadler, *Salesman*, p. 45.

around the question whether thought or feeling best promotes the purpose of discourse. The desired listeners' reaction seems to hinge upon the balanced use of both a demonstration to the intellect of the feasibility and necessity of certain goals and methods, and upon a wise appeal to the emotions. A speech without emotional appeal is apt to leave an audience more knowledgeable but hardly motivated toward specific action.

Sadler demonstrated the capacity to employ pathetic appeals but may have been too extravagant in their use. However, one may conjecture that an audience of businessmen in the 1920's may have responded more favorably to this approach due to the expanding range of opportunities for mobility and success, and in response to the cultural philosophy of "getting ahead." An awareness of human limitations, physiological and psychological, permitted Sadler to realistically adapt his appeals to the ability potentials of those who attended his lecture. Displaying sympathy for and empathy with the salesman's problems and aspirations, he was able to build upon a careful analysis of his audience. His intelligent understanding of the situation, plus his professional insights, prompted an appeal to the emotions that sparked the facts and statistics with reasonable encouragement and operational inducements.

Logos

Logos, the Greek word meaning reason, account or reckoning, is the term used for the interpretation of persuasion by argument. Aristotle stated:

> ... *so in Rhetoric: the example is a form of induction; while the enthymeme is a syllogism, and the apparent enthymeme an apparent syllogism. "Enthymeme" is the name I give to a rhetorical syllogism, "example" to a rhetorical induction. Whenever men in speaking effect*

persuasion through proofs, they do so either with examples or enthymemes; they use nothing else.[425] *... as for the Maxim, it is to be included under the Enthymeme.*[426]

Lawson made this statement concerning the speaker and his auditor: "Everything which seems to contribute to the well - being of the individual is liked, whereas those things which thwart that state are disliked."[427]

The ideas that Sadler presented to his audience contained depth; his logical proof supported the greatest issue which confronts mankind -- self - preservation. The examples, enthymemes, and maxims that he employed in his speaking were derived from his philosophy of life.

Sadler rarely quoted authorities as inartistic proof; he relied upon his own credibility for this logical support. After the hometown doctor introduced him as a Fellow of the American College of Surgeons, former professor at the Post Graduate Medical School of Chicago, Chief Surgeon to Bethany Hospital, Senior Attending Surgeon to Columbus Hospital, Director of the Chicago Institute of Research and Diagnosis, American Medical Association, Member of the Chicago Medical Society, the Illinois State Medical Society, the American Public Health Association and the author of ten medical books [at the time he delivered this speech he was accepted as an authority in his field.

Aristotle mentioned two primary types of enthymemes: the demonstrative through which we draw a conclusion from consistent propositions, and the refutative through which we draw

---

[425] The Rhetoric of Aristotle, I. 2. 1356^b
[426] Ibid., II. 20. 1393^a
[427] John Lawson, *Lectures Concerning Oratory* (Dublin: George Faulkner, 1758), p. 155.

a conclusion from inconsistent propositions.[428]

Sadler implemented demonstrative enthymemes, examples, and maxims in his speech, "What Every Salesman Should Know About His Health." He employed the following enthymemes drawn from the *topos* of opposites. "You feel bad when there is no danger; you feel in fine shape when you are standing on the brink of ruin."[429] He urged his auditors to have a complete physical check - up once a year. "You fellows all know enough to go to your dentists once a year to have your teeth looked into but, you have not been educated to go to your doctor once a year to have your blood, urine, and blood pressure checked up."[430]

He told the salesmen that because of gland endowment some men have more pep than others and gave the following example:

> *Some people are blessed with a well - working ductless gland system ... and find it easy to overwork ... they awaken in the morning surcharged with pep, endowed with indomitable energy. Others from birth, are doomed to suffer from underactivity of one of their ductless glands, and so they must get up in the morning suffering from lack of pep.*[431]

Sadler used an enthymematic chain of opposites as he told his auditors that they must be happy in their job:

> *You have no business to be salesmen if you are not worthy of your own confidence, and you have no business to be selling goods for a corporation, or for anybody, that you cannot believe in. If you don't believe in your own*

---

[428] Rhetoric of Aristotle, II. 22.
[429] Sadler, *Salesman*, p. 86.
[430] Ibid, p. 87.
[431] Sadler, *Salesman*, p. 27.

> firm, make up your mind tonight that you are going to get a new job and make connection with an establishment you can believe in. If you don't believe in your house, then you are doing a great injustice both to the firm and to yourself by going on any further in that state of mind. You will do yourself good and your firm a favor if you will resign...[432]

Sadler continued with a personal experience,

> You know I am a surgeon -- I enjoy my work even though my duties are arduous. Sometimes I am over at the hospital, up most of the night, fixing up people who have busted [sic] their heads in automobile accidents...[433]

Again he used an enthymeme as he advised that they should meet every reaction of their customer with a positive attitude:

> If he breathes pessimism, you counteract with hopeful, sane optimism. You put up a finished fight of salesmanship, designed to convert your subject -- to win him from his viewpoint of indecision and uncertainty to your viewpoint of decision, certainty, and buying.[434]

Throughout the entire speech he reiterated that the salesman must believe in himself; he supported this with enthymemes: "If he doesn't believe in himself, if he doesn't believe in himself, [sic] how can a salesman expect to get out and make people believe in his proposition."[435] When suggesting to the salesman that the customer must believe that he needed the product being sold, Sadler said, "... if you make a suitable approach, if you make a sympathetic contact with him, he will be benefited by doing business with you -- that he will be pleased

---

[432] Ibid, p. 38.
[433] Ibid, p. 110.
[434] Ibid, p. 31.
[435] Sadler, *Salesman*, p. 38.

to become a buyer."[436]

When Sadler suggested the need for proper bowel elimination, he compared the human body to a furnace and once more employed the enthymeme:

> *If you are shoveling in coal three or four times a day, and you only shake the ashes down once every day or two, you cannot keep a fire burning brightly.... Now it is just the same in the case of the human furnace. If you feed your furnace, as some of you do, three times a day -- and between meals -- and then allow your bowels to move only once a day ... you have got to have regular times for cleaning out the human ash box.*[437]

He continued to use the enthymeme as he contrasted elimination with the alarm clock.

> *If you set an alarm for six a.m., allow it to go off, reach out, shut it off, and go back to sleep -- well, you know if you repeat that a number of times you can sleep right through -- you don't hear the alarm clock at all. And that is what has happened in the case of many of you with regard to your bowels.*[438]

Sadler reviewed statistics concerning how many million people die each year prematurely and unnecessarily and then injected an enthymeme drawing from the *topos* of cause and effect.

> *...if we don't do something to stop these people from committing suicide I think the government is going to intervene some day and stop this needless and premature slaughter of its citizens.*[439]

---

[436] Ibid.
[437] Ibid, p. 90.
[438] Ibid, p. 92.
[439] Sadler, *Salesman*, p. 92.

> *I think it is but a short time now when, every time an American citizen dies under fifty years of age, a coroner's inquest will be held in order to determine the cause of death and fix the moral responsibility for dying at such an early and immature age.*[440]

As Sadler discussed the lack of iron in the blood, he described by the use of an enthymeme how blood is tested:

> *If we prick the lobe of your ear with a needle, and take a drop of your blood on a sheet of white paper, allow it to dry for a moment, we can estimate the amount of iron present in an individual's blood, in percentage. If it stacks up with the general average we say the hemoglobin is 100 per cent, or maybe 95 per cent, and in most sedentary people over thirty years of age we find it down as low as 90 per cent. If his hemoglobin is below 80 per cent it is pretty serious, and if it is 75 per cent we say you have some form of anemia - you are a sick man ... if your test shows up 90 per cent or below, what are you going to do about it? ... If your hemoglobin is 80 or 85 per cent you are going to feel no good...*[441]

Sadler demonstrated how the members of the audience could self administer a thyroid test. In so doing, he again resorted to the enthymeme:

> *Take the skin on the back of your left hand and pinch it up into a ridge by taking hold of it between the thumb and forefinger of your right hand. Hold the skin up in this position for a few seconds and then let go quickly ... If this little fold of skin which you have pinched up and stretched away from the back of your hand returns instantly to its normal position, if it shows that it is highly elastic and the rebound is exceedingly quick, that means you have a normally active -- or possibly an over*

---

[440] Ibid, p. 51.
[441] Ibid, pp. 71 - 72.

> - active -- thyroid gland. On the other hand, if this fold of skin which you have pinched up between your thumb and finger returns slowly, sluggishly, and exhibits little or no elasticity, it means that you are sub - thyroid -- that your thyroid gland is under - functioning.[442]

Aristotle said the maxim is "a statement about those things which concern human action, about what is to be chosen or avoided in human conduct," however, he cautioned orators, "the use of maxims is suited to speakers of mature years, and to arguments on matters in which one is experienced."[443] Aristotle added:

> One great advantage of maxims to a speaker arises from the uncultivated mentality of an audience. People are delighted when he succeeds in expressing as a general truth the opinions they entertain about special cases ... People like to hear stated in general terms what they already believe in some particular connection.[444]

This speech included a number of maxims used to augment statements of concern. For example, "master the art of living with yourself as you are and the world as it is";[445] "we must get it into our heads not merely that the world owes us a living, but that we owe the world a life";[446] "Moss doesn't grow on the well side of a tree. Moss grows on the shady side of a dead or dying tree";[447] and, "whatever a man soweth that shall he also reap, sooner or later.[448] These maxims emphasized Sadler's admonitions against intemperate living. Another maxim reinforced the argument that men ought to enrich their lives

---

[442] Sadler, *Salesman*, p. 96.
[443] The Rhetoric of Aristotle, II. 21. 1359ª
[444] Ibid, II. 21. 1359ᵇ
[445] Sadler, *Salesman*, p. 42.
[446] Ibid, p. 51.
[447] Ibid, p. 68.
[448] Ibid, p. 69.

by being open - minded to the viewpoints of others: "That man is well educated who, each day he lives, gets one more man's viewpoint of life."[449]

When the theme turns toward matters of religion, Sadler apprised his auditors that "our life down here is but one short, brief career."[450] He incorporated the maxim, "Our race is soon run, and our earthly goal - death - is soon reached."[451]

Aristotle explained *logos* further by stating that there were two kinds of argument of example: the one being a parallel from the facts of history and the other being a parallel invented by the use of fables, or comparison.[452] Sadler used the fable when he urged the salesmen to have "stick-to-it-iveness." "But it's the same old story of the race between the hare and the tortoise -- the turtle won out while the rabbit slept."[453]

He used an example of comparison as he told his audience that only activity insures happiness: "Now, this successful, energetic salesman ... feels good, having satisfied his salesmanship appetite, just as the drug fiend is blessed with a feeling of satisfaction when he has been able to get his favorite dope."[454] Sadler implemented several examples drawn from medical science; he used factual medical opinion in explaining the ductless gland system:

> *There are six or eight of these glands distributed around through the body ... these half dozen or more ductless*

---

[449] Sadler, *Salesman,* p. 46.
[450] Ibid, p. 116.
[451] Ibid, p. 117.
[452] Rhetoric of Aristotle, II. 20.1393ª
[453] Sadler, *Salesman,* p. 21.
[454] Sadler, *Salesman,* p. 28.

> glands (also called endocrine glands) ... limit the whole domain of so - called personality... [455]
>
> Our conduct is largely determined by fluctuations in pressure -- disturbances in equilibrium -- between these different systems of internal secretion. [456]

He used another example of medical fact as he compared the human blood pressure to a steam engine's gauges and safety valves:

> I have already told you that you have about a thousand miles of blood vessels. Connected with these is the human heart -- a pump that beats incessantly from the cradle to the grave. You men here tonight who are around twenty to twenty - five years of age should have a blood pressure of about 120 millimeters of mercury, and so we say that the average or normal blood pressure for adult men is about 120. You can easily vary 10 degrees. As you get older your blood pressure goes up one point for every two years' increase in age, so that if your pressure is 120 when you are twenty it would be 135 when you are fifty, and that would be considered normal blood pressure for that age. [457]

In order to qualify his belief that mental and physical health were juxtaposed, Sadler utilized factual examples as supporting proof for poor circulation.

> I remember a few years back when they had a patient in the hospital they wanted me to operate on. They said she had goiter. I went in and looked the woman over. Her hands were as cold as ice, and I said, "No, I won't operate on her. She's got hysteria." There is more poor

---

[455] Ibid, p. 23.
[456] Ibid, p.26.
[457] Ibid, p. 82.

> circulation to be charged up to nervousness than to any other one cause.[458]

He quoted statistics for supporting proof as he talked about the sex problem and venereal diseases:

> I don't believe you fully appreciate what a risk a man takes when he so far forgets his good taste and so far loses his self - respect as to consort with scarlet women. Three - fourths of all immoral women have got one or more venereal diseases. Over four million people in this country at the present time have syphilis. Gonorrhea alone causes over fifty per cent of all surgical operations performed upon the female pelvis, and it is responsible for twenty - five per cent of all the blindness in this country. Specialists in this line believe that there are over five million cases of gonorrhea in this country at the present time. Of the eight hundred thousand young men who reach maturity every year in this country, sixty per cent, four hundred and forty thousand, contract syphilis or gonorrhea before they are thirty years of age.[459]

Sadler resorted to further statistical information as he informed his audience that their way of living caused premature death.

> During the past thirty years the mortality from these old - age diseases has nearly doubled in the United States, and it should be remembered that these premature breakdowns are not due entirely to overwork -- they are more largely the result of over - worry and chronic poisoning.[460]

Sadler's ideas and modes of argument were logically harmonious. The evidence used at one point in the speech was always

---

[458] Sadler, *Salesman*, p. 82.
[459] Ibid, p. 125.
[460] Ibid, p. 87.

congruous with the evidence adopted at another point. Primarily, he depended upon his personal authority for expert medical opinion; rarely did he quote others. It was his speaking style to support each assertion with three or four forms of proof. The factual medical example and the personal illustration were applied consistently. When supporting a medical assertion in germane instances, he turned to the enthymeme and maxim. Throughout the speech, the analogy, comparison and contrast, and the antithesis were employed for attention - getting and mnemonic devices.

The outstanding characteristic of the speech to salesmen is the utilization of the language of everyday life. Sadler thus avoids the "cardinal sin" mentioned by Aristotle by refraining from the use of a specialized terminology or professional parlance. His style and usage displays a consciousness of the audience's emotional and intellectual capabilities; his phraseology and examples were individualized for the particular group of auditors.

The pathetic appeal of this speech was directed toward three basic needs: the need for self - preservation, the need for esteem, and the need for self - actualization. Although considerable efforts to effect persuasion by appeal to the emotions are exhibited, the speech rests primarily upon logical proofs to support its main theme. The use of the syllogism is found in each of the arguments presented. This technique demonstrates sound organization as well as oratorical finesse.

Inclusion of numerous clichés – "milk of human kindness," "lame ducks," "blue Monday," "booze," "hootch," and "come in, the water is fine" -- may be a questionable stylistic device but would have some merit if the purpose was to prompt the satisfaction of recognition in a large audience. The same conclusion may be reached concerning the use of maxims. In addition, such devices suggest a closer identification of the speaker with the audience.

It was, of course, in the use of personal examples from his former experiences that Sadler accomplished the greatest identification with his listeners. Using this leverage, he was able to advance his appeal on the basis of affinity and shared insights. This identification plus the professional status of the speaker contributed to the ethical appeal underlying the entire address. Sadler's *ethos* was further enhanced by his conversational style and unpretentious language.

The fourth and fifth canons of rhetoric, *memoria* [memory] and *pronunciatio* [delivery], are also essential in effecting persuasion. Quintilian claimed that memory may be "called the treasure - house of eloquence."[461] Chautauqua audiences preferred speakers who were not tied to their manuscripts or notes. Sadler himself spoke of his unique memory whereby words seemed to appear in his mind as if in print. His daughter reflected that he was "quite dramatic, walked around a lot, got so funny that he would have people in stitches; he was a real entertainer."[462] Former students also underscored Sadler's freedom from notes and a memory that was filled with information, illustrations, and humorous anecdotes. This has received detailed treatment in Chapter II and will not be elaborated upon any further in this chapter.

Sadler was small in stature; however, he had a strong, firm speaking voice. He was a distinguished - appearing individual with attractive, friendly facial features. His delivery was conversational rather than stentorian.

---

[461] Butler, *Quintilian*, XI. 11. 1 - 2.
[462] Christy Interview.

VI. SUMMATIONS AND CONCLUSIONS

Summations

This study was designed to analyze rhetorically those elements of William S. Sadler's speeches on preventive medicine which governed his oral contributions to the American people between 1905 and 1906. In this critical process the methodology employed provided a division of the subject into the traditional rhetorical components of the orator, the occasion, the audience, and the speech.

The historical-critical approach was followed. This led to a survey of the health conditions prevalent in the United States during this period. It led also to an investigation of the typical audience brought together by the circuit Chautauqua. Upon this background, the career of William S. Sadler was traced. Of special importance to the entire study was the review of those biographical facts and personal experiences which prompted him to make public speaking a major outlet for the communication of his ideas and beliefs. Finally, one of his frequently delivered speeches was examined for its rhetorical significance.

A brief review of the findings introduced in this study will demonstrate the rationale for the research. This summary will also emphasize those aspects of the research upon which same of the conclusions that will follow are based. By today's standards, the average American of seventy years ago lacked many of the advantages which are now taken for granted. In an age prior to the widespread use of the automobile and before public broadcasting, Americans were limited in mobility and in their access to sophisticated information. This was especially true in the rural and small town communities. At a time when considerable changes were taking place in the field of medicine and health care, the available channels for the dissemination of such information were quite restricted. Local newspapers could not be relied upon for accurate guidelines in matters of health. Other reasons were to be found in the structure of the medical profession itself. On the one hand, medical training was still elementary and to an undetermined degree -unregulated, and, on the other hand, the American Medical Association, in its attempts to upgrade the profession, restricted any kind of activity such as public speaking which suggested self - advertising. This left the public exposed to unqualified quacks and promoters of patent remedies more interested in profits than in public health. It was apparent that the needs of the people could best be met by medical practitioners who had access to the latest medical insights and to the profession itself.

In 1906, William S. Sadler, newly graduated from medical school, announced his decision to carry the message of health to the people. He believed that the general public was not being informed about health care and that people were being subjected to incorrect information. It was his strong conviction that too little emphasis was being placed upon preventive medicine while too many people, because of their ignorance, were being led into promiscuous use of drugs.

In the years following his decision, Sadler was to find himself speaking from lecture platforms all over America and crowding the spare moments of his busy medical career with similarly motivated efforts to put his message into print. The task which he imposed upon himself was simply stated; however, it called for extraordinary dedication, patience, and ability.

This was a significant decision in several respects. It was, first of all, not the usual choice of a medical doctor, and there were few precedents for this type of activity within the medical profession. To some degree, it called for the courage and c. It was significant also in that it called for some attitudinal change on the part of the medical profession or else the decision may have jeopardized his professional status. Finally, it was a significant resolution because it placed a reputable physician before great numbers of people, a physician who was sincerely concerned about their health and welfare.

A testimony to his decision and to the difficulties encountered in pursuing his mission is implicit in his own statements. On one occasion he said that sometimes he felt like "shutting up like a clam instead of utilizing the effort it took to instruct the laity." But his purpose refused him this relaxation. He believed that there was danger in a minimum amount of incorrect information and it was the responsibility of the competent teacher to give "authentic information" to the layman.

The availability of the Chautauqua and Lyceum organizations with their ubiquitous lecture platforms attracted this young doctor with a message. After convincing the program managers that audiences would welcome the health lectures he proposed, Sadler began a long association with these distinctive purveyors of culture. Sadler contributed to the character and substance of Chautauqua history; in turn, the style of life which was Chautauqua impressed itself upon his life and career.

The lecturer was the main feature of Chautauqua programs. He provided the information and inspiration to millions of auditors and was the source of much public opinion in the communities of America. From its beginning in 1874 to its disappearance in 1932, the Chautauqua institution was heralded as the people's university. Although it was advertised as a free platform, the evidence indicates that its basic philosophy was religious and conservative, and its message was a carefully guarded reinforcement of the Mother-Home-Heaven ideals.

The literature testifies to the fact that Sadler was a popular lecturer. He had the capacity to hold an audience for hours at a time. This was no small accomplishment considering the conditions which prevailed when Chautauqua audiences gathered. Summer heat, distractions caused by the children, occasional stray animals, and frequent storms were but a few of the apparent difficulties encountered by the orators. Sadler used histrionics, demonstrations, and cleverly spaced humor to keep attention.

Many men of national prominence became Chautauqua orators: six presidents of the United States along with college professors, eminent clergymen, doctors of philosophy, lawyers, scientists, authors, travelers and artists were some of the many persons who provided Chautauqua talent. Lecturers, however, had to pass the test of acceptability; a critical indicator of popularity was the requests for return performances. It was relatively easy to get on the platform; it was more difficult to remain there. Sadler frequently had as many return assignments as new ones.

Chautauqua audiences evaluated the *ethos* of a lecturer on the basis of their own life style and attitudes. They subscribed to the principles of hard work, Christian morality, and success in the face of hardship. Sadler apparently passed these tests. When he was being introduced, the audiences would hear of his busy career as a physician and surgeon, professor, author, and traveling lecturer. They would be told that he was careful to abide by the ethics of the medical profession and that he represented no cult or fad. Local physicians respected him and often introduced him to the Chautauqua audiences.

Sadler's message concerning disease prevention found receptive audiences. Often, he would be held over for hours as the auditors plied him with questions indicating their need for more information in matters of health. While being as helpful as possible he nevertheless did not violate his professional ethics by giving individual diagnosis or treatment. He *was* always careful to refer people to their local doctors.

Some of Sadler's efforts were directed at the reform of the Chautauqua institution itself. It was his desire that the health interests of people attending Chautauqua programs should be a foremost consideration of those responsible for such items as ventilation, sanitation, food preparation, and audience comfort. He pointed out the health hazards of such large gatherings and demanded corrective measures.

Recurrent themes in Sadler's lectures centered about the proposition that one should learn the basic laws of nature especially as they applied to prevention of disease and the curative powers of the human body. He emphasized the importance of correct mental attitudes, for it was his contention that "mental mischief" was a basic cause of much emotional conflict as well as many physical illnesses. This latter theme reflected Sadler's intense interest in the workings of the human mind. He was to actualize this interest by his studies with Freud in Vienna in 1911 and by his subsequent entrance into the fulltime practice of psychiatry.

According to associates, Sadler maintained a schedule of unrelenting activity. However, by his diligent attention to essentials and his promptness in dealing with details, he was able to meet the demands of his practice, his lecturing, and his writing.

It is apparent that Sadler's lecturing and writing activities were but two channels for the same message. Many of his books are identified by the author as outgrowths of his health lectures. Some of these were prompted by demands of Chautauqua audiences for printed copies of his lecture materials. A series of health books resulted. Sadler allowed the profits from sales of such books to go to the support of local Chautauquas. More technical books were produced for men of various professions, especially physicians and clergymen.

His preparation for all this activity can be traced back to influences in his early youth. He had been guided and encouraged by those who had insights into his potential. Sadler's public speaking career began with a high school commencement address when he was but eight years old. His college career which brought him under the influence of Dr. John Harvey Kellogg offered formalized training and helped to set the direction of his career. There are strong indications that Dr. Kellogg's role was a significant one because he himself was an outstanding medical doctor and humanitarian.

Sadler's speech text reveals that his speaking was consistent with the best in classical rhetorical theory and practice. In terms of the *dispositio, electio,* and *inventio* of the representative speech, "What Every Salesman Should Know About His Health," Sadler can be placed in the focus of the classical rhetorical tradition. He organized his speeches in the traditional manner; the exordium was brief; transitions and internal summaries were lucid. Although the body of the speech would be regarded as excessively long for a modern audience, it should be remembered that audiences were accustomed to two - hour speeches. Sadler arranged the body of the speech in an order that was easy to follow.

The internal composition of Sadler's speech shows a sensitivity to audience needs. The selection of supporting materials, the elimination of medical jargon, the colorful metaphors, the trite clichés and maxims had appeal for the people of his day.

He practiced simplicity of style; yet his speaking reflects literary competence. His use of ornamentation contributed to his aim and objective by reinforcing his theme, "preventive medicine." His sincerity and faith in his cause was evident as he utilized personal illustrations of his experiences as a salesman. His rhetoric was distinguished by strong *ethos, pathos,* and *logos,* but he was able to rise to pathetic eloquence because of the self - preservation appeal.

The style of the man was perhaps more important than the style of the speech. Sadler had the ability of inweaving a humorous twist; his entire speech sparkled with a display of wit and comic tension release. He had the talent for infusing his delivery with an appropriate display of histrionics and theatricality. It was his manner, word choice, tonality, patterns of communication, warmth of personality-, imposing appearance, strong voice, complete command of himself and of his material that made him a popular lecturer.

Intimate associates of Sadler's describe the dual nature of his personality. Off the platform he tended to be reserved, introvertive - even shy. He did not enjoy "small talk;" however, on the platform he exhibited warmth, friendliness, and self - confidence. On the stage he was an extrovert. He had a dynamic manner of delivery. Rarely using lecture notes, he moved about the platform and with great confidence and enthusiasm proceeded to captivate his audiences.

Conclusions

The speech critic must exercise care in assessing the historical impact of any one speaker or speech. It is misleading to attribute to a subject's ability those consequences which would have occurred with or without his particular contributions. For example, the historical period in which Sadler's speaking career was realized was a time of great transition; many forces were at work. In technology alone revolutionary changes were taking place and were transforming the entire society. Medical science breakthroughs of the nineteenth century were being widely dispersed as were improved delivery systems for health care. The American Medical Association deserves much credit for increasing the skill and improving the integrity of the medical profession.

The orator. It must be remembered, however, that the justification for this study of William S. Sadler was not based upon specific historical consequences of his public oratory but upon the fact of his uniqueness as a medical man who chose public speaking as a conveyance for propagating the message of health. This justification has been supported by the facts.

Sadler illustrates through his efforts the importance of oratory in a democratic society. He had the zeal of a reformer. Not content with things as they were, he attempted to do what he could to change them. In so doing he challenged some traditions and opened new avenues of service; He was a tireless communicator. One may only guess at the actual numbers of individuals who were affected by his message. While one may attribute his popularity to his wit and humor and his ability to entertain, it seems unlikely that his countless auditors, including doctors and ministerial students, were not convinced by the message of preventive medicine.

From all the evidence gathered in this research several conclusions may be reached. First, Sadler's rhetorical effectiveness was primarily based upon factors of personality and character which were revealed in his style. He loved the profession of medicine, and he thoroughly enjoyed speaking to large audiences. Totally immersed in his work he gave no reason to suspect either his motives or his sincerity. Second, his persuasive techniques were well adapted to the audiences of his day. His speeches display no airs of condescension; his respect for the audience is implicitly given. Third, while his message was serious in intent and content, he had the ability to wrap it in an entertaining style and deliver it in such a manner as to hold his auditors' attention and interest. This was his greatest asset as an orator.

Finally, evidence is indicative that Cato's requirement that the orator be "a good man skilled in speaking," is personified in Chautauqua's medic orator, William S. Sadler.

The occasion. For the purposes he had in mind, the Chautauqua platform afforded Sadler the best opportunity to extend the message of health. It would have been impossible to reach as many people in any other manner. By availing himself of the Chautauqua reputation and organization, he was able to reach a cross-section of the American public and especially to appear before the citizens of small towns and rural communities. As an attested force in the molding of public opinion, it was a logical channel for Sadler's reformative influence.

Although Chautauqua standards circumscribed its message with a conservatism and religious morality, such confinements did not interfere with Sadler's presentations. In fact, the nature of his message was well suited to this type of atmosphere.

The audience. The didactic lecture was well received by Chautauqua audiences. Eager for sophistication, oriented toward hard work and self-improvement, defensive of their moralistic views, these audiences could be very critical and demanding. Lecturers who misread the audience and failed to make the necessary stylistic adaptation found themselves ineffective and unpopular. Sadler could personally illustrate the very themes which had appeal to these people. Actually, the success of his message and his reputation as an orator stemmed from his ability to identify with his audiences. It is possible that a prolonged exposure to the audiences of the Chautauqua circuits would produce habits of style and delivery which would be ineffective before other types of audiences. Some of Sadler's books, for example, lack literary style because they appear to have been written for the Chautauqua audience. Much of the oratory of Chautauqua platforms would be anachronistic today.

The speech. The analysis of a typical speech indicated that Sadler was a competent speaker who employed rhetorical techniques effectively and astutely. As a speaker he revealed certain natural gifts: an understanding of human nature, empathy with his auditors, liveliness and readiness of thought, a good memory, and a capacity for close reasoning. He also had acquired skills which served his purpose well. He had a wide range of knowledge and an eclectic approach to experience and learning. A skilled and respected physician and surgeon, he could speak with authority in matters of medicine.

In an individualistic style Sadler used metaphors, allegories, epigrams, and clichés to excellent advantage. The speech, "What Every Salesman Should Know About His Health," was more than the title suggested, for in addition to being a call for improved health habits, it was also an apologia for honesty, industry, and virtuous living.

Recommendations

Areas of special interest to the student of Public Address which were suggested by the research involved in this study can be placed in two categories: those topics related to the Chautauqua institution and its place in American history, and those topics related to the medical profession.

Although much has been written about the Chautauqua institution and its contributions to American oratory, some areas appear to have been neglected. For example, the war oratory of World War I seems to have been one of its important propaganda efforts. Its advocacy of the prohibition movement deserves further investigation and appraisal. A study of the recurrent themes which characterized the Chautauqua presentations might reveal speakers' attempts to relate their messages to the Chautauqua audiences. The residual effects of Chautauqua's influence could possibly be brought to focus by a series of interviews of former patrons.

An obvious neglect of oratory in the medical profession as a subject for research and analysis suggests that that area may provide many opportunities. Other doctors who followed public speaking careers either on the Chautauqua platform or elsewhere could become suitable subjects. The public speaking which advocated the organization of the American Medical Society would have historical and rhetorical significance. One topic more directly suggested by this paper is the ethical code forbidding public speaking by doctors. An in-depth study of this subject and all its implications for the profession as well as for the public could have merit.

BIBLIOGRAPHY

A. PRIMARY SOURCES

1. Papers and Letters

Chicago Institute of Physiologic Therapeutics. Personal correspondence between William S. Sadler and Harry P. Harrison, October 4, 1910, October 10, 1910. Talent file, Redpath Collection.

Chicago Institute of Physiologic Therapeutics. Personal correspondence between Dr. William S. Sadler, Director, and Harry P. Harrison, Manager of Redpath Bureau, October 4, 1910, October 11, 1910, October 13, 1910.

Chicago Institute of Physiologic Therapeutics. Personal correspondence between William S. Sadler and Harry P. Harrison, January 1, 1911. Talent file, Redpath Collection.

Chicago Therapeutic Institute. Personal correspondence between Wilfred C. Kellogg and Harry P. Harrison, September 21, 1917. Talent file, Redpath Collection.

Chicago Therapeutic Institute. Personal correspondence between William S. Sadler, Director, and Harry P. Harrison, March 18, 1918.

Headquarters of the International Lyceum Association. Personal correspondence between William S. Sadler, Chairman, Convention Program Committee, and Harry P. Harrison, Manager of Redpath, February 14, 1911.

Redpath Chautauqua and Lyceum Bureau. Personal correspondence between Harry P. Harrison, Manager, and William S. Sadler, October 11, 1910. Talent file, Redpath Collection.

Redpath Chautauqua and Lyceum Bureau. Personal correspondence between Harry P. Harrison, Manager, and William S. Sadler, January 6, 1911.

Redpath Chautauqua and Lyceum Bureau. Personal correspondence between Harry P. Harrison, Manager, and William S. Sadler, January 26, 1911.

Redpath Chautauqua and Lyceum Bureau. Personal correspondence between Harry P. Harrison, Manager, and William S. Sadler, February 15, 1911.

Redpath Chautauqua and Lyceum Bureau. Personal correspondence between Harry P. Harrison, Manager, and William S. Sadler, February 23, 1911.

"Memorial Service for Dr. William S. Sadler with Dr. Meredith J. Sprunger and Alvin L. Kulieke Officiating."

Sadler, William S. Personal Papers. MSS in office and home, 533 Diversey Parkway, Chicago.

The Sadlers Popular Health Lectures. Chicago: W. N. King Printing Service. Program brochure.

2. Periodical Articles

Sadler, William S. "Are You Committing Suicide On the Installment Plan?" *American Magazine,* CXI (March, 1931), 73.

_____. "Are You Over - Working Your Conscience?" *American Magazine,* CIII (March, 1927), 48 - 49.

Sadler, William S. "Can We Really Stop Worrying?" *Ladies Home Journal,* XXVIII (September, 1911), 21 - 22.

———. "Cause and Cure of Colds," *Parents Magazine,* VI (January, 1931), 24, 60 - 61.

———. "College Women and Race Suicide," *Ladies Home Journal,* XXXIX (April, 1922), 39.

———. "Curing Sick People. Without Medicine," *Ladies Home Journal,* XXVIII (August, 1911), 17 - 18.

———. "Dinner Table Is No Place for Speed or Endurance Records," *American Magazine,* C (November, 1925), 58 - 59.

———. "Do People Get On Your Nerves?" *American Magazine,* C (October, 1925), 24 - 25.

———. "Don't Fool With Tonics, They May Fool You," *American Magazine,* CVIII (July, 1929), 22 - 23.

———. "For A Long Life in the Lyceum," Part I, *The Lyceumite,* VII and *Talent,* XIX, No. 27 (August, 1909), 10 - 11.

———. "For A Long Life in the Lyceum," Part II, *The Lyceumite,* VII and *Talent,* XIX, No. 29 (October, 1909), 8 - 9.

———. "For Health at the Chautauquas," *The Lyceumite,* VII and *Talent,* XIX, No. 25 (June, 1909), 9 - 12.

———. "Getting Away From the Grind," *American Magazine,* CIII (June, 1927), 29.

———. "Getting Ready For Winter," *American Magazine,* CIV (November, 1927), 62 - 63.

Sadler, William S. "Give Your Audiences Fresh Air," *The Lyceumite and Talent*, III, No. 8 (January, 1910), 9 - 10.

_____. "Headaches," *American Magazine*, CIV (October, 1927), 29.

_____. "How's Your Appetite'?" *American Magazine*, CII (November, 1926), 42 - 43.

_____. "How the Mind Causes and Cures Disease," *American Magazine*, XCVIII (July, 1924), 40 - 41.

_____. "The Influence of the Oxygen Bath. On Blood Pressure," *American Journal Physiologic Therapeutics*, I and II, No. 4 (May, 1910 - December, 1911), 417 - 420.

_____, and Lena K. Sadler. "Joy Killers," *American Magazine*, CI (April, 1926), 29.

_____. "Juvenile Manic Activity," *The Nervous Child*, IX, No. 4 (1952), 363 - 368.

_____. "Lost Your Pep?" *American Magazine*, CVII (March, 1929), 39.

_____, and Lena K. Sadler. "Making a Child What We Want Him To Be," *Ladies Home Journal*, XXVIII (November, 1911), 21, 96, 97.

"Medicine's Week in the Nation," *The AMA News:* The Newspaper of American Medicine (May 12, 1969), p. 1.

Sadler, William S. "Ouch!" *American Magazine*, CII (October, 1926), 24 - 25.

_____ "Pep," *American Magazine*, XCVIII (October, 1924), 29.

Sadler, William S. "The Practice of Preventive Medicine." Speech given at the Sixty - Eighth Annual Meeting of the Illinois State Medical Society at Springfield, May 22, 1918. *Illinois Medical Journal,* XXXIV, No. 3 (September, 1918), 113 - 120.

"The Sadler Lectures: Popular Health Lectures, Unique Slum Lectures," *The Lycewnite & Talent,* V and VI (September, 1907), 2, inside cover.

"The Sadlers: A Whole Chautauqua in Themselves," *Lyceum and Talent,* VI, No. 3 (August, 1912), 51.

Sadler, William S. "Seven Causes of Sleeplessness," *American Magazine,* CI (June, 1926), 41.

_____. "Six Fundamentals of Happiness," *American Magazine,* CI (March, 1926), 36 - 37.

_____. "When Doctors Disagree." Speech given at the 1912 International Lyceum Association Convention, Winona Lake, Indiana, September 6, 1912. *The Lyceum News,* II, No. 8 (September, 1912), 8 - 10.

_____. "Sterilization of the Unfit," *Journal of Criminal Law,* VII (January, 1917), 753 - 757.

_____. "Stop A Minute!" *American Magazine,* XCIX (April, 1925), 46 - 47.

_____. "Stop Coddling Yourself," *American Magazine,* CVIII (September, 1929), 68 - 69.

_____. "Suburban and the City Child," *Suburban Life,* X (February, 1910), 66.

Sadler, William S. "They're Your Feet But Stop Abusing Them," *American Magazine,* CVII (February, 1929), 48 - 49.

??????. "The Treatment of Intestinal Stasis." Speech given at the North Side Branch of Chicago Medical Society, November 8, 1918. Available in *Illinois Medical Journal,* XXXV, No. 2 (February, 1919), 57 - 61.

??????. "Watch Out For Health Fads," American *Magazine,* CII (December, 1926), 47.

??????. "Ways to Work Out Your Own Mind Cure," *American Magazine,* XCVIII (August, 1924), 41.

??????. "We're All Afraid of Something," *Collier's,* LXXXIII (June 15, 1929), 30.

??????. "What To Do At Your Age To Protect Your Health," *American Magazine,* CVIII (August, 1929), 53.

??????. "What Wears Thousands of Us Out," *Ladies Home Journal,* XXVIII (October, 1911), 12.

??????. "What You Need to Know About Your Blood Pressure," *American Magazine,* CI (May, 1926), 46 - 47.

??????. "When You Feel Yourself Corning Down With a Cold," *American Magazine,* CV (April, 1928), 24 - 25.

??????. "Whew! But It's Hot!" *American Magazine,* CII (July, 1926), 26 - 27.

??????. "What You Can Do About Your Heredity," *American Magazine,* CX (November, 1930), 33, 114, 119.

Sadler, William S. and Lena K. Sadler. "Why We Get Fat and What To Do About It," *Ladies Home Journals* XXXVII, Serial Form (Nay, 1920), 37 (June, 1920), 37 (July, 1920), 39 (August, 1920), 91 (September, 1920), 151 - 152.

3. Books

Sadler, William S. *Adolescence Problems: A Handbook for Physicians, Parents, and Teachers.* St. Louis: C. V. Mosby Company, 1948.

_____. *Americanitis - Blood Pressure and Nerves.* New York: The MacMillan Company, 1925.

_____. *Cause and Cure of Colds.* Chicago: Thomas S. Rockwell Company, 1930.

_____. *Cause and Cure of Headaches.* Chicago: American Publishers Corporation, 1938.

_____. *The Chicago Therapeutic Institute: The Reliance Baths.* Chicago: Press of Winship Co., 1916.

_____. *Courtship and Love.* New York: The MacMillan Company, 1952.

_____. and Lena K. Sadler. *Diet and Food Values.* Chicago: American Publishers Corporation, 1938.

_____. *A Doctor Talks to Teenagers.* St. Louis: C-. V. Mosby Company. 1948.

_____. *The Elements of Pep.* Chicago: American Health Book Concern, 1925.

Sadler, William S. *The Essentials of Healthful Living.* New York: The MacMillan Company, 1925.

_____. *The Evolution of the Soul.* Published lecture on the William F. Ayres Foundation. Plymouth Congregational Church, Lasing, Michigan, November 18, 1941.

_____, and Lena K. Sadler. *Growing Out of Babyhood.* New York: Funk and Wagnalls Co., 1940.

_____. *Health Hints.* Chicago: American Health Book Concern, n.d.

_____, and Lena K. Sadler. *How To Reduce and How To Gain.* Chicago: A. C. McClurg & Co., 1920.

_____. *How You Can Keep Happy.* Chicago: American Health Book Concern, 1926.

_____. *Living A Sane Sex Life.* Chicago: Wilcox & Follett Co., 1946.

_____. *Long Heads and Round Heads or What 's the Matter With Germany.* Chicago: A. C. McClurg & Co., 1918.

_____, and Lena K. Sadler. *Mastery of Worry and Nervousness.* Chicago: American Publishers Corporation, 1938.

_____. *Measuring Men.* Chicago: Press of Winship Co., 1917.

_____. *Mental Mischief and Emotional Conflicts.* New York: Funk and Wagnalls Co., 1929.

_____. *The Mind at Mischief.* New York: Funk & Wagnalls Co., 1929.

Sadler, William S. *Modern P5ychiatry*. St. Louis: C. V. Mosby Company, 1945.

_____, and Lena K. Sadler. *The Mother and Her Child*. Chicago: A. C. McClurg & Co., 1916.

_____. *Personality and Health*. Chicago: American Health Book Concern, 1924.

_____. *The Physiology of Faith and Fear*. Chicago: A. C. McClurg & Co., 1912.

_____. *Piloting Modern Youth*. New York: Funk & Wagnalls Co., 1931.

_____. *Practice of Psychiatry*. St. Louis: C. V. Mosby Company, 1953.

_____. *Prescription for Permanent Peace*. Chicago: Wilcox and Follett Co., 1944.

_____, and Lena K. Sadler. *Psychiatric Nursing*. St. Louis: C. V. Mosby Company, 1937.

_____. *The Quest For Happiness*. Chicago: American Publishers Corporation, 1938.

_____. *Race Decadence*. Chicago: A. C. McClurg & Co., 1922.

_____. *The Science of Living or The Art of Keeping Well*. Chicago: A. C. McClurg & Co., 1910.

_____, and Lena K. Sadler. *The Sex Life,* I and II. Chicago: American Publishers Corporation, 1938.

Sadler, William S. *Soul-Winning Texts or Bible Helps For Personal Work*. Chicago: The Central Bible Supply Company, 1909.

_____. *Theory and Practice of Psychiatry*. St. Louis: C. V. Mosby Company, 1936.

_____. *The Truth About Heredity*. Chicago: A. C. McClurg & Co., 1927.

_____, and Lena K. Sadler. *Truth About Mental Healing*. Chicago: American Publishers Corporation, 1938.

_____. *The Truth About Mind Cure*. Chicago: A. C. McClurg & Co., 1928.

_____ *The Truth About Spiritualism*. Chicago: A. C. McClurg & Co., 1923.

_____ *What Every Salesman Should Know About His Health*. Chicago: American Publishers Corporation, 1925.

_____, and Lena K. Sadler. *The Woman and the Home*. Chicago: American Publishers Corporation, 1938.

_____. *Worry and Nervousness or The Science of Self-Mastery*. Chicago: A. C. McClurg & Co., 1914.

B. SECONDARY SOURCES

1. Collected Documents

Independent Chautauqua Collection: Redpath Bureau Office, Kimball Building, Chicago, Illinois.

Keith Vawter Collection: University of Iowa Library, Iowa City, Iowa. Papers of the Redpath-Vawter Chautauquas were presented to the library by the estate of Keith Vawter.

The Redpath Collection: University of Iowa Library, Iowa City, Iowa. This Redpath Collection comprises the papers of the Redpath Chautauquas and the Redpath Lyceum Bureau of Chicago, Illinois. It was donated to the University by Harry P Harrison, former manager of the the Redpath Bureau.

Thornton Collection: University of Iowa Library, Iowa City, Iowa. Dr. Harrison J. Thornton, former professor of History did extensive research on the History of Chautauqua. His papers were presented to the library by Mrs. Thornton.

2. Letters, Questionnaires, and Bulletins

Allin, Ronald T. Chagrin Falls, Ohio. Personal correspondence between Mr. Allin and the writer.

Board of National Missions of the United Presbyterian Church in the United States of America. Personal correspondence between the Reverend G. Daniel Little, Coordinator of Planning Institute of Strategic Studies, and the writer, May 13, 1970.

"Bulletin to Talent," Redpath Chautauquas, to Atlantic Five-Day Circuit. Handwritten letter to Talent. Miscellaneous Collection, Msc. 150.

Chicago Therapeutic Institute. Personal correspondence between Wilfred C. Kellogg and Harry P. Harrison, Redpath Bureau Manager, September 21, 1917.

Cobb, Robert L., Salt Lake City, Utah. Personal correspondence between Mr. Cobb and the writer.

Department of Mental Health, Central State Hospital. Personal correspondence between Chaplain George F. Bennett and the writer, May 8, 1970.

Didier, Calvin, Detroit, Michigan. Personal correspondence between Mr. Didier and the writer.

Dierenfield, Charles, Newport Beach, California. Personal correspondence between Mr. Dierenfield and the writer. Questionnaire and letter, May 14, 1970.

Dilley, John R., Fairfield, Iowa. Personal correspondence between Mr. Dilley and the writer.

Filson, Charles, Springfield, Illinois. Personal correspondence between Mr. Filson and the writer.

Frank, Donald H., Santa Anna, California. Personal correspondence between Mr. Frank and the writer.

Holt, L. Emmett. "Medical Ideals and Medical Tendencies." Address at the College of Physicians and Surgeons, September 26, 1906. Speech available in *Columbia University Quarterly,* IX, No. 2 (March, 1907), 105 - 117.

Lankton, C. William, Chicago, Illinois. Personal correspondence between Mr. Lankton and the writer.

LaRue, Charles F., McKinney, Texas. Personal correspondence between Mr. LaRue and the writer.

McCormick Theological Seminary. Personal correspondence between the Office of the President and the writer, January 7, 1970.

Mosby, The C. V. Company Publishers. Personal correspondence between Terry H. Green, General Sales, and the writer.

Omerod, The Reverend John W., Toronto, Ohio. Personal correspondence between the Reverend Omerod and the writer.

Ossentjuk, Albert G., Denver, Colorado. Personal correspondence between Mr. Ossentjuk and the writer.

Oster, Ray. "Final Teardown Bulletin Gulf Circuit," *Redpath Chautauquas*, Miscellaneous File - Msc - 150. C. C. Bulletins, pp. 1 - 3.

Oster, Ray of Redpath Chautauqua. Correspondence in a bulletin between Superintendent of Equipment and Warehouse. Redpath Collection, Miscellaneous Collection, 150.

Raymond, Robert E., Waukesha, Wisconsin. Personal correspondence between Mr. Raymond and the writer.

"Redpath Lyceum News Bulletin," *Redpath Lyceum Bureau*, Bulletin No. 1, Miscellaneous Collections, Msc - 150, September 19, 1927.

Redpath-Lyceum - Bureau, "Publicity Letter Bulletin," Cedar Rapids, Iowa. Miscellaneous Collections, Msc - 150. Bulletins.

Roberts, Morgan S., Portland, Indiana. Personal correspondence between Mr. Roberts and the writer.

Sadler, Christy. Personal correspondence between Dr. Sadler's daughter and the writer, November 4, 1969 and February 3, 1970.

Schomacker, Donald E., Kansas City, Missouri. Personal correspondence between Mr. Schomacker and the writer.

Travis, Murray, Tulia, Texas. Personal correspondence between Mr. Travis and the writer.

Vawter, Keith, Manager of the Redpath - Vawter Circuit, in a Speech delivered to the Poor Richard (Advertising) Club, December 8, 1921, at Philadelphia, Pennsylvania.

Woodcock, Lawrence, Blackwell, Oklahoma. Personal correspondence between Mr. Woodcock and the writer.

3. Unpublished Works

Cumberland, William. "A Classification of Circuit Chautauqua Programs and Talent for the Year 1924." Unpublished Master's thesis, State University of Iowa, 1963.

Graham, Donald Linton. "Circuit Chautauqua, A Middle Western Institution." Unpublished Doctor's dissertation, State University of Iowa, 1953.

Homer, Charles F. "Chautauqua People Are Pretty Good." Unpublished Notes, Chautauqua Collection, University of Iowa, p. 9.

Kee, J. Francis. "History of the Clear Lake, Iowa Chautauqua." Unpublished Master's thesis, State University of Iowa, 1939.

Nau, Helen Gladstone. "The Chautauqua in Des Moines County, Iowa." Unpublished Master's thesis, State University of Iowa, 1937.

Oliver, Robert T. "Oratory of Burke, Fox, Sheridan, and Pitt." Unpublished Doctor's dissertation, University of Wisconsin, 1937.

Penner, Jonathan Gunther. "Public Speaking in the Health Reform Movement in the United States, 1863 - 1943." Unpublished Doctor's dissertation, Purdue University, 1962.

Sadler, William S. "Psychiatric Educational Work." Paper read at the Ninety - second Annual Meeting of the American Psychiatric Association, May 4 - 8, 1936, St. Louis, Missouri.

Schwarz, Richard William. "John Harvey Kellogg: American Health Reformer." Unpublished Doctor's dissertation, University of Michigan, 1964.

Tozier, Roy Becker. "The American Chautauqua: A Study of a Social Institution." Unpublished Doctor's dissertation, State University of Iowa, 1932.

Walker, William B. "The Health Reform Movement in the United States -- 1830 - 1870." Unpublished Doctor's dissertation, Johns Hopkins University, 1955.

Wick, Iverne. "The Circuit Chautauqua, 1904 to *1915.*" Unpublished Master's thesis, State University of Iowa, 1938.

4. Interviews

Myers, Martin. Personal interview. December 30, 1969.

Rawson, Anne. Personal interview. December 30, 1969.

Sadler, Christy. Personal interviews. November 1, 1969; December 29, 30, 31, 1969.

Sadler, Leone. Personal interview. December 30, 1969.

Schlundt, Professor K. David. Personal interview. May 25, 1970.

Sprunger, Dr. Meredith. Personal interview. April 24, 1970.

Stotts, Dr. Jack L. Personal interview. December 31, 1969.

5. Periodicals

Alber, Louis J. "Does the Public Want Quality?" *System,* XXXIX (March, 1921), 373 - 375.

_____ "Making Up America's Mind," *The Independent,* XC (June 9, 1917), 475.

_____ "Most Dangerous Subject," *The Lyceum Magazine,* XXVI, No. 4 (September, 1916),. 16.

Albert, Allen D. "The Tents of the Conservatives," *Scribner's,* LXXII (July, 1922), 54 - 59.

"The American Magazine Has Chautauqua Story," *The Lyceum Magazine*, XXXII, No. 2 (July, 1922), 33.

"The Audience Turns Critic," *The Lyceum Magazine*, XXV, No. 4 (September, 1915), 37.

Bailey, Hillary C. "The Business Side of the Platform," *The Lyceum Magazine*, XXX, No. 7 (December, 1920), 15.

Baumgartner, Andreas. "Foreign View of Chautauquas," *Chautauquan*, LI (July, 1908), 244 - 249.

Blichfeldt, E. H. "What a Chautauqua is not," *Chautauquan*, LXVII (August, 1912), 194 - 198.

Bliven, Bruce. "Mother, Home and Heaven," *New Republic*, XXXVII (January 9, 1924), 172 - 175.

_____ "Nearest the Hearts of Ten Million," *Colliers*, LXXII (September 8, 1923), 6 - 7.

Bohn, Frank. "America Revealed In Its Chautauqua," Thornton Chautauqua Collection, p. 18.

"Book Review," *The Outlook*, CXL (August 5, 1925), 501.

Borland, Hal. "Swift Changes: Modern Life Pushing Into the Discard Picturesque Institution That Carried Culture and Entertainment Into Every Crossroads Town the Country Over," Thornton Chautauqua Material.

Bradford, Ralph N. "The Value of Chautauqua," *The Billboard*, XXXVI (March 8, 1924), 1 - 3.

Bray, F. C. "Organization of Circuit Chautauqua," *Review of Reviews,* LXX (July, 1924), 74.

_____ "Social and Ethical Ideas in Summer Assemblies," *Chautauquan,* XLVII (July, 1907), 171 - 177.

Brigance, William Norwood. "Effectiveness of the Public Platform," *Annals of American Academy of Political and Social Science,* CL (March, 1947).

Briggs, Captain Wood. "The Chautauqua Sham," *Haldeman - Julius Monthly* [Girard, Kansas], I (April, 1925), 284 - 288.

Bryan, W. J "Nation - Wide Chautauqua," *Independent,* LXXIX (July 6, 1914), 21 - 23.

Castle, Maria Johnson. "Chautauqua the Intellectual Circus," *Forum,* LXXXVII (June, 1932), 369 - 374.

Chance, G. S. "Keeping the Chautauqua Family Happy," *The Lyceum Magazine,* XXXIII (May, 1924), 32 - 33.

"Chautauqua and Its Founder," *Chicago Evening Post* in *The Literary Digest,* XLVII (1907), 171.

"Chautauqua and Water," *Nation,* CI (August 5, 1915), 168.

"Chautauqua In A Nutshell," *Literary Digest,* LXV (October, 1921), 27 - 28.

"Chautauqua Plans and People," *The Lyceum Magazine,* XXVI (May, 1918), 24, 28.

"Chautauqua Program," Big Stone Lake, South Dakota, July 3 to 9, 1917. "Chautauqua Progress," *The Survey* (April 24, 1920), p. 146.

"Chautauqua Stars," *Everybody's Magazine,* XXXIII (September, 1915), 323 - 324.

Clarke, Redfield. "Chautauqua an American Institution," *Equity,* VII (July, 1922), 20 - 24.

Dalgety, George S. "Chautauqua Contribution to American Life," *Current History,* XXXIV (1931), 39 - 44.

"The Decay of Idealism," *The Lyceum Magazine,* XXXV, No. 5 (September, 1925), 17 - 18.

Detzer, Karl W. "Broadway R.F.D.," *Century,* CXVI (July, 1938), 311 - 317.

Devilbiss, Lydia Allen. "What People Want To Know About Their Health," Part I, *Hygeia,* II (July, 1924), 435-438.

"Did I Make Good?" *The Lyceum Magazine,* XXXII, No. 11 (April, 1922), 11 - 12.

Editorial. "The Value of Farmer's Chautauqua," *Iowa Homestead,* August 24, 1922.

Ellerbe, Alma and Paul Ellerbe. "I Want to Know Club," *Collier's,* LXVIII (September 17, 1921), 13, 24 - 25.

Ellerbe, Alma and Paul Ellerbe. "The Most American Thing in America," *The World's Book,* XLVIII (August, 1924), 441-446.

Ellison, J. Ray. "The Chautauqua Movement in the West," *The Lyceum Magazine,* VIII (October, 1915), 456-457.

Etty, Anne Suhm. "What's Wrong With Chautauqua?" *The Drama,* XIV (March-April, 1924), 213.

"The Evolution of Chautauqua," *Chautauquan,* XXXV (July, 1902), 349—353.

"The Evolution of the Chautauqua System," *Journal of Education,* LXVIII, No. 8 (September 3, 1908), 1, editorial.

Flude, Al. "What the Chautauqua Means To My Home Town," *Farm and Fireside,* in Thornton Chautauqua Material, 8, 36.

Flude, G. L. "Leaven of Chautauqua," *World Today,* XXI (September, 1911), 1120-1121.

"Mr. Flude's Endorsement of the Sadlers," *The Lyceum Magazine,* XXVI (November, 1917), 4.

Frank, Glenn. "The Parliament of the People," *Century,* XCVIII (July, 1919), 401-416.

Gilbert, L. "In Old Chautauqua," *Chautauquan,* LXIII (June, 1911), 50—57.

Gill, C. W. "Chautauqua and the New Books," *Chautauquan,* LXVII (July, 1912), 147—149.

Griffin, Leland N. "The Rhetoric of Historical Movements," *Quarterly Journal of Speech,* XXXVIII (1952), 184—188.

Harvey, Joseph E. "Four Years of Chautauqua," *The Spectator,* I (October, 1909).

High, Fred. "How Chautauqua Has Influenced the World," *Billboard,* XXXI (March 29, 1919), 1.

Holcomb, Walt. "Famous Men I Have Met: How Great Orators Move Their Audiences To Laughter and Tears," Success, February, 1924, pp. 65-66, 108-110.

"How Redpath—Horner Builds Chautauquas," *The Lyceum Magazine,* XXIII, No. 4 (September, 1913), 51—61.

Howard, R. R. "Chautauqua Invades the West," *Sunset,* XL (May, 1918), 49—50.

Howell, D. W. "Assembly Ideals and Practice," *Chautauquan,* LI (July, 1908), 250—259.

_____ "Round Table at the Assembly," *Chautauquan,* LXIII (June, 1911), 60—61.

"Inveterate Chautauqua Fan," *Scribner's,* LXXIV (July, 1923), 119-120.

"Keeping the Chautauqua Family Happy," *The Lyceum Magazine,* xxxiii, No. 2 (May, 1924), 32—33.

Kelly, Fred C. "What 20,000,000 People Like to Hear," *American Magazine,* LXXXVII (June, 1919), 32—33, 104—106.

Kennedy, Bart. "Audiences the World Over," *The Lyceum Magazine,* XXVI, No. 2 (July, 1916), 21.

Kennedy, H. H. "The Lecturer as a Featured Attraction on the Chautauqua." Fifteenth Annual Convention of the International Lyceum Association, *Yearbook,* vii (September 15—20, 1917). Miscellaneous Records 150, Chautauqua Collections.

Lucey, Thomas E. "Chautauqua, The Show With A Conscience," *Billboard*, XXIX (March 24, 1917), 31, 214.

Lybarger, Lee F. "Struggle for Survival in the Lyceum and Chautauqua," *International Lyceum and Chautauqua Year Book*, VII (1917), 49—51.

"The Lyceum and Chautauqua's Great Opportunity," *The Lyceum Magazine*, xxvi, No. 12 (May, 1917), 10.

MacLaren, Gay. "Morally We Roll Along——To Chautauqua," *The Atlantic Monthly*, CLXI (May, 1938), 673.

Maslow, A. H. "A Theory of Human Motivation," *Psychological Review*, (March, 1943), 382.

Mason; Gregory; "Chautauqua: Its Technic," *The American Mercury*, I, Na. 3 (March, 1924), 275—280.

"Putting the Talk in Chautauqua," *The Outlook*, CXXVIII (July 6, 1921), 418—420.

Matthews, E. L. "Ideals and Cooperation in the Field," *The Lyceum Magazine*, XXX, No. 7 (December, 1920), 15—16.

McCarter, N. H. "In the Heart of Kansas," *Chautauquan*, LIX (July, 1910), 274—280.

McClure, Frank. "The Chautauqua of Today," *Review of Reviews*, L (July, 1914), 53 - 59.

McDonald, A. B. "Tent Universities," *Country Gentlemen*, August 12, 1922, pp. 13 - 15.

"The Message of Health for the Masses," *The Lyceumite & Talent*, III, No. 10 (March, 1910), 32 - 33.

Moon, Otis V. "Chautauqua Over - Advertised?" *The Lyceum Magazine*, XXXII, No. 2 (July, 1922), 27.

Morgan, Frank A. "Discussing the Work and the Workers," *The Lyceum Magazine*, XXXIV, No. 1 (June, 1924), 19 - 20.

Mullinax, Ira D. "Hog Chautauqua? Not a Thing Less," *The Poland China Journal*, August 10, 1918, pp. 64 - 66.

"Notes of the Week," *Saturday Review*, CXVI (September 13, 1913), 317 - 318.

Ott, Edward Amherst. "The Chautauqua Movement," *The Lyceumite and Talent*, XXIII (June, 1913), i.

Pearson, Frank B. "A Close - Up of a Chautauqua Crowd," *The Lyceum Magazine*, XXXV, No. 11 (April, 1926), 5.

Pearson, P. M. "Chautauqua Movement," *Annals of American Academy*, XL (March, 1912), 211 - 216.

Pearson, Paul M. "Some Good Rules for Chautauquas," *The Lyceum Magazine*, XXVI, No. 4 (June, 1916), 18.

"People of the Platform,'~ *Billboard*, XXXVII (May, 1925), 56.

"Personal: Dr. William S. Sadler, Surgeon, Author, and Teacher," *The Lyceumite and Talent*, V, No. 3 (August, 1911), 7.

Platt, Electra. "Mail Order Lessons In Platformology or Platforming Made Easy," *The Lyceum Magazine*, XXX (December, 1920), 18.

Pound, Louise. "Miscellany: Chautauqua Notes," *American Speech,* IX, No. 3 (October, 1934), 232 - 234.

Powell, Lyman P. "The End of a Perfect Day," *The Outlook,* CXX (September, 1918)~, 103.

Pringle, Henry F. "Chautauqua Creed," *The American Mercury,* XVI (January, 1929), 88.

Pringle, Henry F. "Chautauqua In the Jazz Age," *The American Mercury,* XVI (1929), 85 - 86.

"Publisher's Views on Topics of the Times," *The Iowa Homestead,* Thornton Chautauqua Materials, p. 6.

Redpath, James. "The People's College," *Lyceum and Chautauqua,* XXV, No. 5 (October, 1915), cover.

Schaer, Von Dr. K. F. "Das Anpassungsproblem," *Psychologische Rundschau,* II. Jahrgang, No. 1, Basel (April, 1930), 1 - 3.

Schlesinger, Arthur N. "A Dietary Interpretation of American History," *Proceedings of the Massachusetts Historical Society,* LXVIII (October, 1944; May, 1947), 210.

Schultz, John Richie. "Chautauqua Talk," *American Speech,* VII (October, 1931; August, 1932), 405 - 411.

"Secretary of State and the Chautauqua Circuit," *Outlook,* CV (September 27, 1913), 158 - 160.

Sheldon, C. N. "Task of the Talent," *Independent,* XCI (August 4, 1917), 165.

Shippey, Lee. "On The Chautauqua Circuit," *Colliers,* LII (November 29, 1913), 20 - 26.

Short, Wallace. "Letter to the Editor," *Labor Magazine,* December 6, 1924, p. 4. Vawter Collection.

Slosson, E. E. "The Chautauqua Idea," *The Independent,* LXXXVI (1916), 251.

Smith, Clay. "How to Get a Start in Chautauqua," *Etude,* XL (September, 1922), 591 - 592, 598.

Smith, Roy L. "Human Nature on the Chautauqua Circuit," *The Christian Advocate,* September 11, 1924, pp. 1105 - 1106.

Strother, F. "Great American Forum," *World'sWork,* XXIV (September, 1912), 551 - 564.

"Summer Assemblies for 1905," *Chautauquan,* XLII (October, 1905), 188 - 194.

Tarbell, Ida N. "A Little Look at the People," *Atlantic Monthly,* CXIX (May, 1917), 602 – 610, 197.

Thompson, Carl D. "Is Chautauqua a Free Platform?" *New Republic,* XLI (December 17, 1924), 86 - 88.

Thornton, H. J. "Chautauqua in Iowa," *Iowa Journal of History,* L (April, 1952), 97 - 122.

Tozier, R. B. "A Short Life - History of the Chautauqua," *The American Journal of Sociology,* XL, No. 1 (July, 1934), 72 - 73.

Treadwell, Louise. "Playing Chautauqua Stands," *The New York Times Magazine,* October 29, 1922, pp. 1 - 4.

"Uplift of Chautauqua Week," *Literary Digest*, XLVII (October 18, 1913), 684 - 685.

Vaughn, Arthur Peirce. "Circuit Riding With the Big Brown Tops," *The Continent*, XLIX, No. 35 (August 29, 1918), 969 - 970.

Vincent, Bishop John H. "The Chautauqua," *The Lyceum Magazine*, July, 1910; November, 1910, on cover.

Vincent, Elizabeth. "Old First Night," *The New Republic*, XL (September 24, 1924), 95 - 97.

"What Anti - Prohibition Lecturers Forget," *The Lyceum Magazine*, XXXIV, No. 1 (June, 1924), 31 - 32.

"When You Have Lost Your Audience," *The Lyceum Magazine*, XXVI, No. 7 (December, 1916), 30.

Wiggam, Albert Edward. "Is the Chautauqua Worthwhile?" *The Bookman*, LXV (1927), 339 - 406.

Wile, Frederick William. "Chautauqua Through Journalistic Eyes," *The Lyceum Magazine*, XXXIII, No. 9 (February, 1923), 23 - 24.

Wilson,. Alonzo E. "The Temperance Chautauquas," *The Spectator*, May, .1909, pp. 8 - 9.

Wilson, Edna Erle. "Amusement a La Carte," *The Designer and the Woman's Magazine*, February, 1923, pp. 30, 52.

_____ "Canvas and Culture," *Outlook*, CXXXI (August, 1922), 598 - 600.

"Wolf Broth for Arthritis," Time, November 24, 1940, p. 71.

Zielinski, Mary V. "Culture Under Canvas," *The Iowan Magazine,* XV, No. 3 (April 15, 1967), 12 - 13.

6. Books

The AMA News. Publication of the American Medical Association, Nay 12, 1969.

Anderson, Martin P., Wesley Lewis, and James Murray. *The Speaker and His Audience.* New York: Harper & Row, 1964.

Aristotle: Poetics, VI, trans. William Hamilton Fyfe. London: W. Heinemann, Ltd., 1932.

Aristotle's Poetics & Rhetoric, ed. T. A. Moxon. New York: E. P. Dutton, 1934.

Auer, J. Jeffrey. *An Introduction to Research in Speech.* New York: Harper & Row, 1959.

Bonner, Thomas Neville. *Medicine in Chicago, 1850 - 1950.* Madison: The American Historical Research Center, Inc., 1957.

The Book Review Digest, VI, No. 12, January - December. Minneapolis, Minnesota: H. W. Wilson Co., p. 347.

Bormann, Ernest G. *Theory and Research in the Communicative Arts.* New York: Holt, Rinehart and Winston, Inc., 1966.

Brigance, William Norwood (ed.). *A History and Criticism of American Public Address.* 3 vols. New York: Russell & Russell, 1960.

Brigance, William Norwood. *The Spoken Word.* New York: F. S. Crofts & Co., 1929.

Burrow, James G. *AMA: The Voice of American Medicine.* Baltimore: Johns Hopkins Press, 1963.

Case, Victoria and Robert Ormond Case. *We Called It Culture: The Story of Chautauqua.* New York: Doubleday and Company, Inc., 1948.

Cicero De Oratore, I, II and III, trans. E. W. Sutton and H. Rackham. Cambridge: Harvard University Press, 1942.

Clough, Caroline Louise. *His Name Was David.* Washington, D.C.: Review and Herald Publishing Association, 1955.

Conant, James B. *Modern Science and Modern Man.* Garden City: Doubleday and Co., 1952.

1846 - 1958 Digest of Official Actions. 1st ed., I. American Medical Association, 1959, 670.

Dunne, Edward F. *History of Illinois*, III. Chicago: The Lewis Publishing Company, 1933.

Emerson, Ralph Waldo. "Man the Reformer," *Nature, Addresses, and Lectures.* Vol. I of *The Complete Works of Ralph Waldo Emerson.* Boston: Houghton, Mifflin, 1884.

Evans, James W. and Harding Gardner L. *Entertaining the American Army, the American Stage and Lyceum in the World War.* New York: The Association Press, 1921.

Flexner, Abraham. *Medical Education in the United States and Canada.* New York: Carnegie Fund for the Advancement of Teaching, 1910.

Franklin, C. Benjamin. *Handbook of Information and Instruction: Associated Chautauquas of America*, No. 50. Redpath Collection.

Garceau, Oliver. "Morals of Medicine," *The Annals of the American Academy of Political and Social Science*, CCCLXIII, January, 1966.

Gunung, John Franklin. *The Working Principles of Rhetoric*. Boston: Ginn and Company, 1900.

Gould, Joseph E. *The Chautauqua Movement*. New York: State University of New York, 1961.

Guthrie, Douglas. *A History of Medicine*. Philadelphia: J. B. Lippincott Co., 1946.

Harrison, Harry P. and Karl Detzer. *Culture Under Canvas: The Story of Tent Chautauqua*. New York: Hastings House, 1958.

Hart, Albert B. *America at War: A Handbook of Patriotic Education References*. New York: National Security League, 1918.

Hillbruner, Anthony. *Critical Dimensions: The Art of Public Address*. New York: Random House, 1966.

Hochmuth, Marie K. (eds). *A History and Criticism of American Public Address*, III. New York: Longmans, Green, 1955.

Hollingworth, H. P. *The Psycholo- of the Audience*. New York: The American Book Company, 1935.

Homer, Charles F. *Strik₀ The Tents: The Story of the Chautauqua*. Philadelphia: Dorrance & Company, 1954.

Index and Digest of Official Actions: American Medical Association Beginning with the Year 1904. Chicago: American Medical Association, 1942.

The Institutio Oratoria of Quintilian, trans. H. E. Butler. 4 vols. Cambridge: Harvard University Press, 1958.

Isocrates, Antidosis, trans. George Norlin. 3 vols. London: W. Heinemann, Ltd., 1929.

Knight, Marian A. and Mertice M. James (eds.). *The Book Review Digest,* XXI. New York: H. W. Wilson Co., 1926.

Lawson, John. *Lectures Concerning Oratory.* Dublin: George Faulkner, 1758.

MacLaren, Gay. *Morally We Roll Along.* Boston: Little, Brown and Company, 1938.

Marsh, George Perkins. *Lectures on the English Language.* New York: Scribners, 1863.

Nay, Henry F. *The End of American Innocence: A Study of the First Years of Our Times, 1912-1917.* New York: Knopf, 1959.

Nowry, George Edwin. *The Twenties: Ford's Flappers and Fanatics.* Englewood Cliffs, N. J.: Prentice - Hall, 1963.

Murry, J. Middleton. *The Problem of Style.* London: Oxford University Press, 1922.

Oliver, Robert T. *History of Public Speaking in America.* Boston: Allyn and Bacon, Inc., 1966.

Orchard, Hugh A. *Fifty Years of Chautauqua, Its Beginning, Its Development, Its Message and Its Life.* Cedar Rapids, Iowa: The Torch Press, 1923.

Parkes, Henry Bamford and Vincent P. Carosso Crescent. *America: A History.* Book One: *1900 - 1933.* New York: Thomas Y. Crowell Co., 1963.

Thaedrus, The Works of Plato, I, trans.-Henry Cary. London: J.M. Dent & Sons, Ltd., 1854.

Pickard, Madge E. and Carlyle Buley. *The Midwest Pioneers: His Ills, Cures, and Doctors.* New York: Henry Schuman, 1946.

Plato, ed. and trans. Lane Cooper. London: Oxford University Press, 1938.

Plato's Dialogues, trans Benjamin Jowett. Oxford: The Clarendon Press, 1892.

The Poetics of Aristotle, Its Meaning and Influence, ed. Lane Cooper. New York: Cooper Square Publishers, Inc., 1963.

Principles of Medical Ethics of the American Medical Association. Chicago: Medical Association Press, 1903.

Quaal, Ward L. and Leo A. Martin. *Broadcast Management.* New York: Hastings House, 1969.

Quintilian's Institutes of Oratory, I and VI, trans. J. S. Watson. London: G. Bell and Sons, 1913.

The Rhetoric of Aristotle, trans. Lane Cooper. New York: D. Appleton and Company, 1932.

Richmond, Rebecca. *Chautauqua, An American Place.* New York: Duell, Sloan and Pearce, 1943.

Sanford, William P. *English Theories of Public Address, 1530-1828.* Columbus, Ohio: Harold L. Hedrick, 1931.

Scott, Marian. *Chautauqua Caravan.* New York: D. Appleton - Century Company, 1939.

Sigerist, Henry, M.D. *Civilization and Disease.* Ithaca, New York: Cornell University Press, 1944.

_____. *Landmarks in the History of Hygiene.* London: Oxford University Press, 1956.

_____. *Medicine and Human Welfare.* Terry Lectures at Yale University. New Haven: Yale University Press, 1940.

Some Chautauqua Facts. Chicago: The University of Iowa Chautauqua Collections, Msc - 150, Miscellaneous Programs, Redpath Chautauquas.

Tefft, Benjamin Franklin. *Webster and His Masterpieces.* 2 vols. Buffalo: Orton & Mulligan, 1854.

Thomlinson, Ralph. *Population Dynamics: Causes and Consequences of World Population Change.* New York: Random House, Inc., 1965.

Thonssen, Lester and A. Craig Baird. *Speech Criticism.* New York: The Ronald Press, 1948.

Through the Meshes. Cleveland: W. C. Tyler Company, 1922.

Twenty Years of Chautauqua Progress: 1904-1923. Cedar Rapids, +

The United Presbyterian Church in the United States of America, Part III, The Statistical Tables and Presbytery Rolls, Seventh Series, Vol. II. Philadelphia: Office of the General Assembly, 1969.

Vollmer, Howard M. and Donald L. Mills (eds.). *Professionalization.* New Jersey: Prentice - Hall, 1966.

Who's Who in America, 1950 - 1951, XXVI. Chicago: The A. N. Marquis Company, 1950.

Who's Who in The Midwest. Chicago: The A. N. Marquis Company, 1949.

Yeager, Raymond and Jerald L. Banninga. *A Speaker's Guide to Syllogistic Reasoning.* Dubuque: Wm. C. Brown Co., 1967.

7. Newspapers

The American Mercury, September, 1928.

The Burlington Hawkeye [Iowa], June 3, 1928.

"Chautauquas as a New Force in Politics," *Indianapolis News,* September 9, 10, 11, 12, 16, 1908.

"Chautauqua Liked By Millions," *New York Times,* July 12, 1914.

Devlin, Joseph. "Lecturing While the Mercury Boils," *New York Tribune,* August 19, 1923.

"Dr. W. Sadler Services Are Planned Today," *Chicago Tribune,* April 29, 1969.

"Dr. William S. Sadler," *Chicago Daily News,* April 28, 1969. Editorial. *The Chicago Evening Post,* September L9, 1916. Editorial. "Fifty Years of Chautauqua," *Des Moines Tribune,* October 28, 1922.

Editorial. "Lyceum and Chautauqua," *Chicago Evening Post,* September 19, 1916.

McDonald, A. B. "Chautauqua, the People's University,-" *Kansas City Star,* June 7, 1934.

New York Tribune, September 20, 1925.

Outlook, August 5, 1925. "Sadler Obituary,' *Chicago Tribune,* April 29, 1969.

8. Other Sources

Taylor, Ruth H., Hackensack, New Jersey. Personal correspondence between Mrs. Taylor and the writer, November 2, 1970.

VITA

G. Vonne Meussling was born July 23, 1926 in Fort Wayne, Indiana. She received a Bachelor of Arts degree from Lakeland College, Sheboygan, Wisconsin in 1948. From 1952 to 1961 she was a teacher and a supervisor in the Niles Public Schools, Niles, Michigan. In 1954 she was graduated from Western Michigan University with the Master of Arts degree.

In September, 1963, she became an Instructor of Speech at the Indiana Institute of Technology in Fort Wayne, Indiana. After teaching in that appointment for five years, she obtained a sabbatical leave to enter the doctoral program in the field of Speech at Bowling Green State University, Bowling Green, Ohio.

About the Author
(2017)

When we arrived at the home of Dr. Vonne Meussling to talk to her about the idea for this book, we were expecting to meet a 90-year old woman. A radiant, well dressed lady came to the door, and we thought she wasn't nearly old enough to be Dr. Meussling, but it was! As we all chatted, we found out she's a youthful person with a zest for life and laughter, and yes, she really is 90 years old! She told us she has rediscovered some friends from her childhood days in Payne, Ohio, and they now meet weekly for lunch to laugh and talk like the childhood buddies they still are. We found her charming, lovely, and upbeat.

We had a very early draft of this book to leave with her, and when we told her it contained her entire Ph. D. thesis she was very excited. We told her we were hoping to get to know about her and get a nice photo to use in the book. She was thrilled, and we chatted easily for about 90 minutes before it seemed time to say goodbye.

We learned that she was born in 1926 at Lutheran Hospital, Fort Wayne, Indiana, to parents Isetta and Frank Wilcox of Payne, Ohio. Eight years later her brother, Stanley was born. There was also an adopted cousin, who she knew as her older brother, Ed. Together, their family had an active farm life. When asked about the family farm she recalls:

> [We had] livestock, crops, both - complete farm... pigs – my father would never let me get near the pigs. He wouldn't let me feed the pigs, but I could feed the chickens and the turkeys. My mother hatched eggs for the Kuck's Turkey Farm, and I would help her turn those eggs. Boy did she work hard. Farm women really work hard. Yep, just the other side of Payne Ohio, we've still got the farm.

> ... Oh it was such a thrill when I was allowed [to drive the tractor]! And then I was forced to drive the tractor ...
> I had to do farm work you know. But I never was allowed to milk the cows because my father got kicked by a cow and had to go to the Mayo Clinic, and so I was never allowed to. But I love the country. You can take the girl out of the country but you can't take the country out of the girl!
>
> I had a wonderful mother and father. I adored my mother with every fiber of my being. And I begged her to let me go to college. I begged her. And so, my father did what my mother wanted, so that's how I got to go to Mission House.

Mission House was at that time the name of a seminary in Wisconsin, now known as Lakeland University. She received her Bachelor of Arts degree in 1948. The University took over the campus of Mission House in 1962, and the Seminary relocated to Minneapolis/St. Paul, becoming United Theological Seminary of the Twin Cities.

During these early years, she met her first husband, a minister, and they built a beautiful house back on the family farm, where her four children (Stephen, Mark, Vonne, and Todd) were born and grew up. After 25 years of marriage her husband died, and then, sadly, she lost her oldest son, Stephen to Leukemia at 30 years old. She reminisced with affection about their home's 3 fireplaces, and how lovely a place it is. She recalled working during the day and getting up at 2 a.m. to work on her thesis when they lived there. She even approached the current owner about buying it back, but they weren't ready to sell at that time. Now, she says, she's happy where she is - in her beautiful house in a suburban subdivision, near her son and her friends - and probably wouldn't move back, even if she had the chance.

She pointed to her many beautiful pieces of antique furniture and told us:

> As a minister's wife we had no money, so what did I do? I'd go to auctions. And my mother loved auctions. I would go to auctions and buy old furniture and refinish it. It was my life blood and breath, refinishing this furniture.

In 1968, after being employed at Indiana Institute of Technology for about five years, Vonne Meussling was granted a sabbatical to attend Bowling Green State University to obtain her Ph. D. in the field of Speech.

> I LOVE Indiana Institute of Technology. They gave me a sabbatical. I only had a Masters. Indiana Institute of Technology -- which is here now, it's in Fort Wayne, and, I taught there -- the President gave me a sabbatical with half salary to get my Ph. D. - and I had four kids, so that wasn't easy. Oh, my. That was rough. I'd get up at 2 a.m. because I worked at the time, see. But I couldn't say no, you know - to get a sabbatical with half salary, so I had to get it with four kids. And I went to Bowling Green, and I tell you I would cry, I'd miss my kids so much. And my mother would say – my mother lived next door because it was our farm - and she said "Don't you cry! I'll take care of those kids." [here Dr. Meussling laughed, remembering].

> I'd come home on weekends. But I couldn't do it anymore, because I had to clean up house, and feed the kids, and do all that .... And my mother'd say "No, you stay over there, I'll take care of those kids."

We asked Dr. Meussling how she arrived at the idea to do her thesis on Dr. Sadler. It turns out that the idea was given to her by Fort Wayne, Indiana, minister Dr. Meredith Sprunger.

> *Meredith Sprunger was a pastor, when my first husband was living. That's how I knew him, he was an Evangelical Reform minister, which is now called the United Church of Christ. I never liked it when they changed that name, I liked Evangelical Reform. Yeah, that's how I knew the Sprunger's. I knew Meredith more than I knew his wife. He was certainly a wonderful guy. He's the one that told me to write about Sadler ... I was in communication you see, and [Sadler] was a medic orator. And so I went to Chicago to visit [Sadler's] daughter [Christy] because he was already gone. She was so lovely, to tell me everything about Dr. Sadler. She was the one that told me so much. She was very accepting, very helpful when she talked about him. And I just thought that was wonderful. So that's why I did it. I traveled all over to get information. Even Chautauqua New York!*

Meredith Sprunger was a name very familiar to us because of his connection to the *Urantia Book*. He was actually another of our wonderful contacts as we researched our own first book. He was known in the Urantia community for being one of the original ministers to whom Dr. Sadler presented the *Urantia Book* upon its completion, and Dr. Sprunger was a teacher and advocate of the Urantia material for the rest of his life. So we asked Dr. Meussling if she ever read the *Urantia Book*.

> *Well, I certainly read parts of it. I didn't read it all. And it was a great thing.*

She told us she had attended some of the Urantia study group meetings held at Dr. Sprunger's home. Each time we mentioned his name she reiterated what a wonderful man she thought he was.

After visiting for some time, we asked Dr. Meussling about her plans for the future. As if this thought wasn't new to her, she told us she thought she'd love to be teaching again, but it wasn't something her husband, Carl, wanted her to do now.

INDEX

A

Adler, Alfred, 3
Alber, Louis J., 85, 92
American Medical Association
  and medical lectures, 3, 14, 16, 45, 50
  code of ethics, 3, 9, 14, 16, 21, 43
  improvements to medical profession, 51, 183
Americanitis (high pressure living), 17, 18, 36, 47, 84, 113, 114, 120, 121, 193
Aristotle, 75, 139, 147, 148, 150, 154, 155, 164, 165, 166, 170, 171, 174, 213, 217
Auditors (see also, 27, 71, 86, 101, 102, 103, 104, 111, 112, 117, 118, 122, 128, 133, 136, 138, 146, 149, 152, 159, 165, 166, 171, 174, 178, 180, 183, 184, 185

B

Bell, Alexander Graham, 76

C

Chautauqua
  appeal of, 10, 87, 104
  audience (see also, 18, 82, 84, 89, 110, 111, 119, 121
  conditions of, 179
  contracts, 80
  contribution of, 10
  decline of, 95, 99, 178
  ethics of, 87, 89, 112, 148
  influence, 95
  management, 27, 80, 89, 94, 95, 112, 126, 127, 134, 148
  morality, 89, 90, 93, 95, 96, 179, 184
  origin, 94, 95, 178
  patriotism of, 92, 93
  Redpath-Chicago circuit, 18, 74, 78, 81, 188, 197, 198, 199, 218
  Redpath-Horner circuit, 93
  showmanship, 102
  speakers, 86, 89, 93, 94, 112, 120, 148
    Carnegie, Dale, 135
    U.S. Presidents, 86, 179
    variety of, 87
  speakers:, 86, 179
  speech length, 111, 136, 149
  the people's university, 178
  the poor man's university, 85
  topics, 74, 87, 96, 109, 131, 135
  travel issues, 82
Chicago Medical Society, 15, 16, 66, 165, 192
Cicero

teaching on oratory, 143, 144, 145, 146, 147, 152, 153, 159

E

Education
standards of society, 10
Emerson, Ralph Waldo, 75, 107, 108, 153, 214

F

Flesch (formula for readability), 145
Freud, Sigmund
beliefs, 160
image, 131
on deepest human urges, 160
Sadler rejected some of his theories, 38
Sadler's teacher, 3, 19, 180

G

Genung, John F.
on motivation, 160, 164, 174
on proper language, 157
Goodrich, Dr. Chauncey A., 155, 156
Greeley, Horace, 76

H

Health
cleanliness, importance of, 11
education, 18, 19, 22
life expectancy, 11
nurtitional aspects, 22

I

International Medical Missionary and Benevolent Society, 34

J

James, Henry, 76
James, William
criticism of Chautauqua, 98
on deepest human urges, 160
on motivation, 160

K

Kellogg, John Harvey, 22, 32, 34, 35, 37, 201
founder of the Chicago Medical Mission, 34
Kellogg, William K., 33

L

Lowell, James Russell, 76

M

Maslow, A.H., 161, 208
Medicine
preventive medicine, 3, 9, 13, 17, 20, 22, 30, 45, 51, 52, 105, 106, 127, 176, 182, 183
quackery, 12, 20
reforms to, 13, 22, 183

safety of, 12
  unregulated practice of, 12

N

Newspapers
  significance of, 10

Q

Quintilian (on rhetoric), 136, 138, 140, 141, 148, 152, 175, 216, 217

R

Redpath, James, 76, 77
  founder of modern Lyceum movement, 76, 77

S

Sadler, Lena K. (wife of William S.), 19
Sadler, William S.
  and Seventh Day Adventist Church, 33
  and Young Men's Intelligence Society, 34
  as psychiatrist, 180
  as salesman, 33, 136
  as speaker, 17, 18, 21, 32, 83, 109, 136, 149
    composition of speeches, 137, 181
    humor, 4, 56, 57, 58, 59, 62, 63, 101, 117, 138, 160, 163, 175, 179, 182, 183
    influence, 183
    style, 61, 62, 63, 64, 147, 182, 183
  as surgeon, 112, 136
  as writer, 17, 83
  associated with
    Adler, Alfred, 3
    Freud, Sigmund (see also Freud, Sigmund), 3
    Jung, Karl, 3
    Kellogg, John Harvey, 3
  birth, 31
  declined university position, 17
  his laws of nature, 102, 113, 116, 117, 118, 180
  influences, 26, 118
    Cicero, 26, 54, 141, 143, 144, 145, 146, 147, 152, 153, 159, 214
    Kellogg, John Harvey, 181
    Quintilian, 136, 138, 140, 141, 148, 152, 175, 216, 217
  lectures
    copies of, 134
    to women, 102, 132
  motivation, 21, 83, 122, 178
  on preventive medicine, 3, 9, 17, 30, 46, 106, 107, 114, 177, 180, 191
  on sleep, 118
  slogan, 136, 142
  student of Sigmund Freud, 19
  student of Sir Berkley Moynahan, 19
  support of local Chautauquas, 181
  The Life Boat magazine, 34

theory of mind cure, 20, 118, 119, 180
words as effective therapy, 20

Speeches
best qualities of for a speaker, 148
construction of, 148

T

Thoreau, Henry, 76

V

Vawter, Keith
manager of Redpath—Vawter circuit, 79, 86, 88, 97, 197

Related Titles

EDGAR CAYCE AND THE URANITA BOOK

By John M. Bunker and Karen L. Pressler

ISBN 978-0988500181

About the time of his Chautauqua career, Dr. Sadler became involved with the process of creating the *Urantia Book*, a masterpiece of thought-provoking and high-minded material that is revered all over the world. The origins of the book remain shrouded in mystery. *Edgar Cayce and the Urantia Book* presents a well-researched collection of facts that may help to unravel the mystery.

www.ingramcontent.com/pod-product-compliance
Lightning Source LLC
Chambersburg PA
CBHW071913160426
43198CB00011B/1281